Flowering Trees & Shrubbery

Lawn

Flowering Trees & Shrubbery

Lawn

Lawn

Lawn

Flowering Trees & Shrubbery

Flowering Trees & Shrubbery

The Labyrinth
of
New Harmony
Indiana

A volume in the Hyperion reprint series
THE RADICAL TRADITION IN AMERICA

THE LABYRINTH

THE ELM AND THE LABYRINTH

The Labyrinth

A history of the New Harmony Labyrinth, including some special study of the spiritual and mystical life of its builders, the Rappites, and a brief survey of labyrinths generally.

By

ROSS F. LOCKRIDGE

Director of the New Harmony Memorial Commission, in collaboration with other members of the Commission.

HYPERION PRESS, INC.
Westport, Connecticut

Published in 1941 by the New Harmony Memorial Commission, New Harmony, Ind.
Hyperion reprint edition 1975
Reproduced from a copy in the collection of the Ohio State University Libraries
Library of Congress Catalog Number 75-336
ISBN 0-88355-239-6
Printed in the United States of America

Library of Congress Cataloging in Publication Data

Lockridge, Ross Franklin, 1877 - 1952.
  The labyrinth.

  (The Radical tradition in America)
  Reprint of the 1941 ed. published by the New Harmony
Memorial Commission, New Harmony, Ind.
  Bibliography : p.
  1. Labyrinths. 2. Harmony Society. I. Indiana.
New Harmony Memorial Commission. II. Title.
HX656.N5L78   1975   335'.9772'34   75-336
ISBN 0-88355-239-6

CONTENTS

ILLUSTRATIONS

The diagram of the Labyrinth used in the cover design was prepared by
H. J. Schnitzeus and Hugh A. Sprague.

The inscriptions (pages 93-4) were selected by consensus of a representative
group of New Harmony people and drawn on the panels of the temple by
Hugh M. Phillips of Poseyville, Indiana.

Preface

THIS brochure is the second of a series of official publications by the New Harmony Memorial Commission. The first, *The Old Fauntleroy Home*—a book of 231 pages—was published in 1939. It is a full presentation of that particular unit in New Harmony and contains also some of the historic background of the community as viewed from the portals and windows of the Old Fauntleroy Home.

Each of the series of publications is devoted to some outstanding unit of the Memorial with all the historic associations that attach to it. Some duplication is necessary in order that each publication may be a fairly complete unit. There is some repetition in this brochure for the sake of emphasis in presenting different phases of various subjects from special points of view.

The attempt is made in this brochure to show the place of labyrinths in the world generally as well as to illumine all the associations of the Labyrinth of the Harmony Society in connection with the distinctive character of the Harmonists. This involves detailed explanation of all those significant features of their lives and customs that may throw light upon the Labyrinth as symbolical of their spiritual conceptions and the mystical tendencies of some of their leaders.

The subject matter has been drawn from many sources. The pages of literature, history, and mythology have been scanned widely for all kinds of miscellaneous references to labyrinths. Valuable assistance was given by the New Harmony Library, the Library of Indiana University, and the Indiana State Library. Special aid was received from the Library of Congress and the Smithsonian Institution.

The most thorough and authoritative work on labyrinths is the book, *Mazes and Labyrinths*, by W. H. Mathews, which has been used extensively. It is a very comprehensive account of the history and development of labyrinths generally containing many source data and original illustrations.

PREFACE

Of contemporary source records, the *Diary* of William Owen and the *Journal* of the Duke of Saxe-Weimar have been especially helpful. William Owen, the second son of Robert Owen, came with his father to Harmonie on the Wabash in December, 1824, and remained there until the Rappites left some five months later. He kept a rather elaborate diary during all that time. The Duke of Saxe-Weimar spent some time both in New Harmony, Indiana, and in Economy, Pennsylvania, in the spring of 1826.

For intimate data concerning the Harmony Society, invaluable help has been received from John S. Duss of Ambridge, Pennsylvania. Most of his life, both in early childhood and maturity, has been spent in old Economy (Ambridge, Pennsylvania)—much of it within the Harmony Society. He conducted the schools of the Society, was a member of the Board of Elders and its last male trustee, serving from 1890 to 1903. Mrs. Duss, who became mistress of the Great House in Economy after the death of Gertrude Rapp in 1889, succeeded her husband as sole trustee in 1903 and dissolved the Society in 1906. Mr. and Mrs. Duss now live in the Great House, which was the home of George and Frederick Rapp.

The rare little book, *Thoughts on the Destiny of Man, Particularly with Reference to the Present Times,* by the Harmony Society in Indiana in 1824, has been quoted freely. It may be regarded as the embodiment of their religious and social creed. Although it was published anonymously, it is known to be the work of George Rapp. Dr. Karl J. Arndt of Louisiana State University, who has made research during the summers of 1940-41 into the archives of the Harmony Society now preserved at old Economy, has found that this book was written by George Rapp. He wrote it after a very thorough study of all of the works of the German philosopher, Herder, who died in 1803, the year that Rapp came to America. All of Herder's works are in the Great House Library.

Father Rapp drew upon the humanitarian philosophy of Herder for the spiritual basis of his practical development of a working Christian brotherhood in the Harmony Society. The *"Thoughts"* of Rapp are closely akin to the *"Ideen"* of Herder. He wrought constructive

PREFACE

"Harmonie" out of Herder's idealistic *"Humanität."* Thus, Rapp became the practical executor, whereas Herder dealt only with theory.

Rapp developed a successful practice. The *"Thoughts"* that he set out in this little book were exemplified almost perfectly in the actual experience of the Harmony Society on the Wabash. Consequently, this book is of immeasurable value in its authoritative exposition of the underlying principles of the Harmony Society—the harmonious combination of practicality and spirituality, of work and worship.

The assistance of high school English teachers throughout Indiana in making research for literary references to labyrinths, or mazes, is gratefully acknowledged. The outside front cover was designed by Mrs. Frederick G. Balz, President of the New Harmony Memorial Commission, who was a former art teacher. She helped also in determining the artistic arrangement of all the illustrations. Mrs. Balz and other members of the Commission, especially Mrs. Edmund Burke Ball and Miss Helen Elliott, have given helpful counsel and assistance throughout the preparation of the brochure.

Representatives of the Pennsylvania Commission now engaged in the restoration of old Economy have given timely assistance. Some leaflets and brochures of Economy, including the little history of The Harmony Society by Dr. Aaron Williams, have contributed to the light and color that were derived from first-hand contacts there. Source data and source excerpts have been used extensively. These source words should be pondered thoughtfully. They contain the essence of the treatise.

. . . . to and fro
caught in a labyrinth you go.
—*Cowper.*

What is this mighty labyrinth—the earth,
But a wild maze the moment of our birth?
—*British Magazine for 1747.*

O! the fetterless mind! how it wandereth free
Through the bewildering maze of Eternity!
—*Henry Smith.*

If you go into a labyrinth, take a clue with you.
—*Old Proverb.*

Foreword

THE Labyrinth was one of the unique features of old Harmonie on the Wabash. Its restoration by the New Harmony Memorial Commission marks the completion of an important unit in a permanent state Memorial. It is one of the very few formal labyrinths to be found anywhere in the world today.

The Harmony Society, better known in Indiana as the Rappites, expressed their faith and mysticism through the unique horticultural design of the Labyrinth, which passed away soon after them, as truly as they expressed their solidity and thrift in their sturdy buildings that still remain. In connection with their practice of the universal cultivation of fine flowers, it may be assumed that the Labyrinth symbolized their belief in the early coming of the millennium. It also typified their conception of the winding ways of life by which a state of true social harmony was to be attained ultimately. It seems, furthermore, to have been regarded by them and by those who visited them, as a pleasure ground. Thus, it integrated truly the harmony of those devout people.

Labyrinths, or mazes, were rare phenomena of ancient and medieval times—particularly in the Mediterranean states and in middle Europe. By symbolical suggestion, they characterized in an artistic way the spiritual and mystic concepts of great peoples in those early days.

Interesting reflections of labyrinths, or mazes, run through many centuries of history and literature as well as of mythology and folk-lore. All this was well known to the founders of Harmonie on the Wabash in the early part of the 19th century. It is fitting, therefore, that the New Harmony Memorial Movement should symbolize this assemblage of associations by the restoration of the Labyrinth of the Harmony Society and by the publication of this brochure in elucidation of its memorial significance.

It should be understood that somewhat extensive treatment is given in this brochure to all phases of the spiritual life of the Harmonists—

their piety and their mysticism—primarily because it is considered that this is the proper place in the series of Memorial publications for the development of that part of the history of the Harmony Society. It is not intended to express obvious relation in all this to the Labyrinth, although there is surely some symbolical relationship.

This background of knowledge may help to explain or suggest why the Harmonists built and maintained a labyrinth. Anyhow, it may be hoped that through this modest exposition of their spiritual life a better grasp can be had of the significance of the Labyrinth; and that through a study of labyrinths generally, a better comprehension of some of the outstanding characteristics of its builders will be derived. It is a prime objective of the New Harmony Memorial Movement to try to invest this assemblage of associations with all the symbolical significance deserved.

PART I

The New Harmony Labyrinth, Past and Present

WHAT IT WAS

WHEN the members of the Harmony Society left their home on the Wabash in 1825 for their new home in Beaver County, Pennsylvania, they left the Labyrinth in its completed state, fully grown and well maintained as a finished horticultural design. It was an integral part of the community that they had built in that wilderness on the Wabash. As a material unit, it was just as real in its physical proportions as were all the other physical features of a well organized community—churches, community houses, mills, factories, and fort-granary; their substantial dwellings of brick, frame, and log; and their well cultivated fields, orchards, and gardens.

Among all these, the Labyrinth was a distinctive unit of the Harmonie they had built. Very little record has been found, as yet, concerning either its construction or its use, but its very existence expressed its meaning with fragrant significance. Naturally, it had been an object of interest to early travelers who visited that region and the subject of some written comment by them, both during the time when the Rappites were here and for some years afterward. We are indebted to those contemporaneous writers for descriptions of the Labyrinth.

Here are some typical excerpts from those original sources. John Melish wrote of it in 1822, as follows:

> This was a most elegant flower garden with various hedgerows disposed in such a manner as to puzzle people to get into the little temple, emblematical of Harmony, in the middle. The Labyrinth represents the difficulty of arriving at harmony. The temple is rough on the exterior, showing that, at a distance, it has no allurements, but it is smooth and beautiful within to show the beauty of harmony when once attained.

Victor Duclos, who came as a boy eight years of age on the Boatload of Knowledge in 1826 and spent the remainder of a long life in New

Harmony, included in his recollections written at an advanced age the following account of the location of the Labyrinth.

> The brickyard was at about the distance of two blocks south of South Street on the east side of the Mt. Vernon road near where Murphy Park is located.
>
> West of this was the rope walk, west side of the road. This was not enclosed except to protect the machinery. Southwest of this and to the north of the road, leading to the Cutoff River was their Labyrinth. Within a circle of about 140 feet in diameter there were formed concentric circles with growth of hedge plants, presenting an intricate pathway leading to a small block house in the centre. The house was built of wood blocks about twelve inches long pointed at one end. These were placed with the pointed ends outward to form a circular wall. The arrangement was such that it was almost impossible for anyone not accustomed to the construction to find their way to the building or to its interior.

William Owen, the second son of Robert Owen, who came with his father on his first visit to Harmonie in 1824, made the following brief reference to the Labyrinth in his diary, December 18, 1824.

> We walked out to see the Labyrinth, which is now not so beautiful as in summer, owing to the want of foliage, flowers, etc. In the center of it is a house, not locked, yet no one can get into it.

Count Karl Bernhard, better known as the Duke of Saxe-Weimar, who was one of the most distinguished visitors of the Community of Equality in the spring of 1826, mentioned his observation of the Labyrinth in his voluminous journal, April 15, 1826.

> After we had returned to New Harmony, I went to the orchard on the Mount Vernon road to walk and beheld to my great concern, what ravages the frost had committed on the fruit blossoms. The vines must have been completely killed. The orchards planted by Rapp and his society are large and very handsome, containing mostly apple and peach trees, also some pear and cherry trees. One of the gardens is exclusively devoted to flowers, where, in Rapp's time, a labyrinth was constructed of beech tree hedges and flowers, in the middle of which stood a pavilion, covered with the tops of trees.

Perhaps the most illuminating reference to the Labyrinth from those early observers was that of Robert Dale Owen. He came to Harmonie (then New Harmony) with his father on the Boatload of Knowledge, filled with youthful zeal concerning this idealistic setting for his father's new social experiment. In his autobiography, *Threading My Way,* he made the following comment upon the Labyrinth as he saw it and as it had been exhibited to his father by the Harmony Society before he purchased the community from them.

> When my father first reached the place, he found among the Germans—its sole inhabitants—indications of plenty and material comfort, but with scarcely a touch of fancy or ornament; the only exceptions being a few flowers in the gardens, and what was called "The

Labyrinth," a pleasure-ground laid out near the village with some
taste, and intended—so my father was told—as an emblematic representation of the life these colonists had chosen. It contained small
groves and gardens, with numerous circuitous walks enclosed by high
beech hedges and bordered with flowering shrubbery, but arranged
with such intricacy, that, without some Daedalus to furnish a clue,
one might wander for hours and fail to reach a building erected in
the centre. This was a temple of rude material, but covered with
vines of the grape and convolvulus, and its interior neatly fitted up
and prettily furnished. Thus George Rapp had sought to shadow
forth to his followers the difficulties of attaining a state of peace and
social harmony. The perplexing approach, the rough exterior of the
shrine, and the elegance displayed within, were to serve as types of
toil and suffering, succeeded by happy repose.

There are later accounts which may have some contemporaneous
significance, such as the description given by a local historian, J. Schneck,
in a paper presented February 17, 1890, before the Mt. Carmel Historical Society.

The principal vineyards were on the hill sides south and southeast
of the town. Near one of these they had built a summer house surrounded by concentric labyrinthian walks, shrubbery, etc., being
planted in the various openings. They were so arranged, that unless
you took a certain course, the paths would again lead you back to
the entrance without reaching the house. They took great delight in
showing their visitors this puzzle, and having them try to solve it.

What might be taken as an inspired literary interpretation of the
Labyrinth is found in Caroline Dale Owen Snedeker's charming book,
The Town of The Fearless.

At the edge of town was a marvelous Labyrinth. The many circuitous and deceiving paths were hedged with yew higher than one's
head. There were garden patches and flowers for the summer time.
In the center a little eight-sided, "garten-haus" built of tiny eight-
sided blocks, with a door of a single, unbelievable plank, with a
secret lock which no one could open without great contrivance.
Inside was a comfortable and pretty room. It was a Rappite symbol,
made as the old Hebrew prophets used to make their tiny model cities
and then destroy them before the people, saying: "Thus shall your
city be destroyed." The Labyrinth was to say to the people of
Harmonie: "Thus difficult it is, by many paths, to win one's way to
ease and comfort." Surely they listened to the Labyrinth and were
industrious. This Labyrinth, inexcusably destroyed before I came on
the scene, was one of the dreams of my childhood. I used to look
across the green meadow to the grove of locusts which marked its site
and intensely mentally reconstruct it. Had it remained it would have
taught me much.

Katherine Evans Blake, in her novel, *Heart's Haven,* described the
inner temple of the Labyrinth with the freedom of romantic fiction.

The Temple of Harmonie was a characteristic representation of
Rappite mysteries. Rude without, in order to typify the difficulties
and privations through which the human soul arrives at the highest

things, it was furnished within like a Greek temple. It was circular, with white columns standing in a gleaming row, and a white dome swelling upward to a central source of mellow light. The floor was paved with white stone, and in the center of it, with the light striking full upon it, and drawing from it a whiteness to which all the rest was shadow, brooded a marble figure of Silence, with serene face and great wings half-unfurled. The head drooped, and a finger upon the lips awed and soothed the beholder. Upon the base was an inscription in German: "Be still, and know that I am God."

This must be taken as purely imaginative; but it may be thought to reflect true atmosphere and color.

John S. Duss said concerning the Labyrinth at Harmonie on the Wabash, in his notable address at the centennial celebration in New Harmony, June 6, 1914:

A short distance from the village was a famous horticultural design which visitors came miles to see. A Labyrinth of vines and shrubs was constructed about a summer house, rough on the exterior, but beautifully furnished within. Robert Owen, on his first visit, was told this was emblematic of the life the colonists had chosen.

We are fortunate in having such authentic first hand knowledge concerning the Labyrinth of the Harmony Society, leaving little question as to its location and its construction. It was in perfect form when the Owenites came, and we have some records to show that it continued to exist in its natural state for some years afterward, but with little or no attention from the dreamers who followed the founders of Harmonie.

In a letter of William Pelham, written at New Harmony, November 7, 1825, he said:

The Labyrinth has not been destroyed but it has been neglected as of little comparative importance.

A more intimate view of the Labyrinth, as it appeared to a boy of twelve in the days of the Community of Equality (1826), is to be found in the "Brief Notes for Autobiography" of Minor Kilbourne Kellogg, the famous American portraitist. These notes were recently acquired by the William Henry Smith Memorial Library. Kellogg says:

The first Labyrinth I ever saw was at New Harmony. It was grown in an open field near the town, and was a source of constant amusement to children. Its lines were formed of vines grown upon light fences and about four ft high, converging as they reached the centre. Here the visitor came upon a circular hut made of the ends of rough logs cut to a point externally leaving one window—& a blind door which had to be sought out—& only found by pushing at the walls. I remember well my first visit to this hut, after a long & tedious run back and forth through the Labyrinth. On seeking for the door a large snake took a look at me from between the logs, laughing at me with its long red tongue. I got back out of the Labyrinth much sooner and easier than I found my way in. This playhouse had been formed by the ingenious Germans of the Rapp community.

There is also a report in the *New Harmony Gazette* of July 9, 1828, that a part of the program of the Fourth of July celebration in New Harmony, July 4, 1828, was given at the Labyrinth. The newspaper says in its account of the activities of the day that:

> In the course of the morning, Dr. Thompson also delivered in the Labyrinth an oration on the celebration of our national independence, after which, a number of ladies and gentlemen partook of a barbecue under the shade of the adjoining trees.

So it was apparently recognized up to that time as a place of public interest, but there is no evidence that it received any special community attention after the dissolution of the Owenite Community of Equality. We must accept the conclusion that the heterogeneous Owenites in their first dreamy conceptions as to the conduct of a modern Utopia in New Harmony found no correlation of the Labyrinth with their purposes. Apparently, no organization and no individual felt responsible for its preservation. Consequently, no adequate care was exercised over it by anyone, either in the active days of the Community of Equality or in the evanescent afterglow.

So it simply aged out of existence in the inexorable course of nature, just as a beautiful flower garden comes to a melancholy end after the hands that planted it and cared for it pass away. As nearly as can be ascertained, practically all trace of it was obliterated some time between 1840 and 1850. Its disappearance was due mainly to the fact that it had no symbolical significance to the Owenites who succeeded the founders of Harmonie.

However, it may be explained also that this was probably due in part to what may be called the temporary nature of its construction. The fact that the hedge rows were made up of various plants and trees such as beech, dogwood, thorn, etc., made it inevitable that the Labyrinth must soon lose its harmony and symmetry of form. As the trees grew up disproportionately they over-shadowed the shrubs and flowers. Uniformity was impossible, and the beauty of the Labyrinth passed away The wooden block house decayed.

In the passing of the years, the Labyrinth passed also. This carries the natural suggestion that its builders probably had no thought that it would be maintained perpetually. Believing as they did that the millennium was near at hand, there was no reason why they should construct a symbol that would maintain its form and significance for any considerable period of time.

THE LABYRINTH

THE RESTORATION

FOR purposes of restoration, a study was made of all local data in New Harmony and in the Indiana State Library and the Library of Indiana University. Assistance was also given by the Smithsonian Institution and the Library of Congress. Horticultural experts and practical landscape gardeners were consulted and the advice of technical architects obtained. Thus, acting upon the best authority available the restoration has been made by the New Harmony Memorial Commission.

The Commission was very fortunate in being offered a beautiful site perfectly suited for the location of the Labyrinth on ground immediately adjacent to the original Labyrinth of the Harmony Society. In fact, it may be considered a part of the old Labyrinth ground, as it was the connecting area between the Labyrinth and the south orchards and vineyards, leading toward the cut-off of the Wabash, in the direction of Indian Mound and Maple Hill. The ground consists of 225 feet front and 327 feet depth. The major portion of it, known as the elm tree lot, 135 x 327 feet, was donated by Mr. A. Clarence Thomas, an elder citizen of New Harmony. The remaining 90 feet, known as the peony lot, immediately adjoining the elm tree lot on the south, was purchased by the Commission with funds provided by the generosity of one of its members, Mrs. Edmund Burke Ball, who also provided for the construction of the Labyrinth, the temple and the fence, all complete.

The plan is an adaptation of a design provided by John S. Duss. Some complexity was added in harmony with that drawing in order to contribute both mystery and symmetry as a fitting extension of the labyrinthine design. The hedge rows are uniform, consisting mainly of Amoor River privet, which is noted for its hardiness and consistency. The Harmonists had used a kind of wild river privet in their hedge rows, together with flowering trees and shrubs, and some thorn trees, fittingly symbolical of the thorny paths of life. Unfortunately, they were not compatible with permanent symmetry. There will be no want of uniformity and no disproportionate growth in the restored Labyrinth.

The inner temple is constructed of stone taken from the Wabash River not far from the old Rappite dam. Its architectural features were determined after a thorough study of all the descriptions and illustrations of labyrinthine temples that could be found in the Library

The Temple

of Congress. Two members of the New Harmony Memorial Commission, Mrs. Frederick G. Balz and Mrs. Edmund Burke Ball, spent some time in the Library and were given ready assistance. They procured photostatic prints of a wide range of ancient labyrinthine temples that were very helpful in this study.

Later Mrs. Balz made a special trip to Economy at Ambridge, Pennsylvania, and inspected the temple, or grotto, in the Great House garden, which the Harmonists built of huge field stones. It is overgrown with vines, giving it an air of seclusion. From photographs taken of it and from the design and color of the interior, helpful suggestions were derived for modeling the temple in the restored Labyrinth at New Harmony, although it is not in any sense a copy. This temple along with others constructed by the Harmony Society was considered from the standpoint of suggesting the medium of construction of our restored temple, which is made to embody the spirit of all the Harmonist temples. Flowering vines and flower-bearing trees are being cultivated on and around the outside, substantially the same as was done with the old temple of the original Labyrinth in Harmonie.

The arrangement of hedge rows and flowering plants was designed and directed by Henry J. Schnitzeus, Landscape Supervisor of the State Highway Commission of Indiana, assisted by Hugh A. Sprague. This work was done in October, 1939. The plans for the inner temple were made and executed by the architectural firm of Harry E. Boyle & Co. of Evansville, Indiana. The construction work was done by Wells & Sons of Mt. Vernon, Indiana. It was finished in April, 1941.

Thus, the restored Labyrinth represents a substantial reproduction in place and form, and certainly in spirit, of the Labyrinth of the Harmony Society. It will be of a permanent and enduring nature, easily maintained, and with minimum need of renewal as the years pass. With the winding divagations of the hedge rows, the attractive interior of the inner temple, and the beautiful floral decorations, the Labyrinth expresses all the natural and artistic beauty that belongs to labyrinths generally and that belonged especially to the pioneer Labyrinth of the Harmony Society.

The spacious plaza, or esplanade, in front, is shaded by a gigantic historic elm planted there in 1863 by Colonel Julian Dale Owen, son of Robert Dale Owen, while at home on a furlough from the battle fields of the Civil War. The esplanade offers an ideal stage for games and exercises, as well as pageants and public meetings of every nature, suited to the spirit of the Labyrinth.

WHAT WAS THE RAPPITE CONCEPTION OF THE LABYRINTH?

IT is easier to restore the symbol that the Rappites left behind them in the form of a Labyrinth than it is to interpret the significance they saw in it. The very uncertainty surrounding their purpose in building it and their use of it makes it all the more labyrinthian and interesting. All the other monuments that the Rappites left behind them, such as their sturdy buildings, their solemn cemetery, their well cleared fields, their orchards, vineyards, and gardens, speak plainly for themselves and reflect clearly the superb solidity and simplicity of those worthy people. But this was not true of the Labyrinth.

It reflects a spiritual phase of their life and culture that is as mysterious as was the Labyrinth itself. And that is what gives to the restored Labyrinth a compelling lure that is genuinely challenging. This is perhaps its most fascinating feature. It permits and even encourages mental diversion and divagation into the realm of Rappite mysticism, not unlike the wanderings and the illusions that may be enjoyed in the penetration of the Labyrinth itself.

Some interesting light may be thrown upon this study by a consideration of the history of world famed labyrinths, which was as well known to Father George Rapp and Frederick Rapp as it is to us today. Notwithstanding the great responsibility of Father Rapp as patriarch and spiritual head of the Harmony Society, he was a persistent student of science and history, as well as of religion. Every moment of his time that was not occupied directly in the fields and factories and in the preparation of his sermons and in his fatherly ministrations, was devoted to a zealous study of various sciences and history. It is well known that Frederick Rapp, his adopted son and first assistant, was highly cultured and well informed in history and literature, as well as in art and science and in business and government.

It is natural to conclude that the Labyrinth was the production of their combined genius and that they drew upon the vast body of history and mythology surrounding the subject of labyrinths generally for the symbolism to which they devoted it, in connection with the principles of the Harmony Society. Consequently, a brief presentation here of some outstanding phases of that history is pertinent to our study, which will involve also a consideration of the peculiar religious beliefs and spiritual practices of the Harmony Society.

PART II

The Labyrinth in History, Mythology, Literature, and Art

LABYRINTH OR MAZE

THE very name of this horticultural design is invested with elusive and varied meaning suggestive of its mysterious significance. The word "labyrinth" has a widely extended application and has become by usage not only synonymous, but really interchangeable, with the simpler word "maze." The most comprehensive book upon this subject is entitled *Mazes and Labyrinths,* by W. H. Matthews. In the introduction, the author makes the following comment upon these terms:

> What is the difference, it may be asked, between a maze and a labyrinth? The answer is, little or none. Some writers seem to prefer to apply the word "maze" to hedge-mazes only, using the word "labyrinth" to denote the structures described by the writers of antiquity, or as a general term for any confusing arrangement of paths. Others, again, show a tendency to restrict the application of the term "maze" to cases in which the idea of a puzzle is involved. . . . Generally speaking, we may use the words interchangeably, regarding "maze" as merely the northern equivalent of the classic "labyrinth." Both words have come to signify a complex path of some kind, but when we press for a closer definition we encounter difficulties.

A study of the meaning of these words is a pursuit in the realm of etymology and constitutes a mental adventure somewhat akin to the physical feat of threading the labyrinth itself. The origin of the words has less significance than the variations of their usage. Webster's *New International Dictionary* defines labyrinth as follows:

> 1. An edifice or place full of intricate passageways which render it difficult to find the way from the interior to the entrance, or from the entrance to the central compartment; a maze; specifically, in Greek myth, the labyrinth constructed by Daedalus for Minos, king of Crete, in which the Minotaur was confined.
> 2. Any intricate or involved inclosure; esp., a maze of paths in a park or garden. Hence: A representation of such a maze, as in a print, intended as a kind of puzzle, or as inlaid in a pavement (a piece of significant decoration often used in medieval churches).

3. Any object or arrangement of an intricate or involved form, or having a very complicated nature; an inextricable or bewildering state of things, etc.; a perplexity; a maze.

Synonyms—Labyrinth, maze are often used with little distinction. Labyrinth emphasizes the idea of structural intricacy; maze, which often applies to what is shifting, heightens the implication of confusion or bewilderment.

Webster gives a simpler, or shorter, definition of maze:

1. Delirium; delusion; a wild fancy; a confused notion; a deception.
2. Confusion of thought; perplexity; uncertainty; state of bewilderment; amazement.
3. A confusing and baffling network, as of paths or passages; an intricacy; a labyrinth; as, the mazes of philosophy.

Synonyms—See Labyrinth.

Plato used the word, labyrinth, to describe an elaborate argument. In the works of Theocritus, it was applied to fish traps of intricate design. Some light is thrown upon the variety of usage and meaning of the words in classical literature, as seen, for example, in the following lines from well known authors:

> The Labyrinth of the mind. . . . *Tennyson.*
> I' the maze and winding labyrinths o' the world. . . . *Denham.*
> Thou shalt not . . . hear through labyrinth's ears. . . . *Donne.*
> A maze of life and light and motion is woven. . . . *Shelley.*
> Some are bewildered in the maze of school. . . . *Pope.*
> Quaint mazes on the wanton green. . . . *Shakespeare.*
> Love in these labyrinths his slave detains. . . . *Pope.*
> Five miles meandering in a mazy motion. . . . *Coleridge.*

It seems that maze has come to have a somewhat more general application in literature than labyrinth. For example, in Strachey's *Queen Victoria* we find this suggestive use of both words in a single sentence:

> The Prince Consort attempted to thread his way through the complicated labyrinth of European diplomacy and was eventually lost in the maze.

Summing all this up in its relation to our restored Memorial unit, it is evident that both labyrinth and maze may be applied to any complex arrangement of shrubs, or trees, or turf, or grottos, or rooms, or buildings, whereby winding ways lead to uncertain ends and may bring the wanderer out to the place from which he started, or may bring him to some desired goal which he is seeking in the very heart of the maze or labyrinth. Therefore, wherever these words are used in an applied or allegorical sense, they carry the same implication of intricacy or mystery.

Looking at it from any point of view it is to be said that the memorial restoration in New Harmony fills all the definitive requirements of either a labyrinth or maze. It was called the Labyrinth by the Harmony Society, and as its restoration now serves the purposes of an historical memorial, it should be known formally as the Labyrinth today. It should be added here that the inner structure—which in some labyrinths has been designated variously as garden house, pavilion, or temple— should be known in this restored Labyrinth of the Harmony Society as the temple.

THE CRETAN LABYRINTH

(Theseus and the Minotaur)

PERHAPS the best known of all ancient labyrinths was the so-called Cretan Labyrinth, located at Knossos on the Island of Crete. In well established mythology it was built there by the iron-breasted King Minos in the days when Crete was the most powerful of the Mediterranean states. This hard-hearted tyrant employed Daedalus, who was a renowned inventor and engineer, to construct the labyrinth for the housing of the Minotaur, a hideous monster having the head of a bull and the body of a man. In revenge upon Athens, for the alleged murder of his son Androgeos in Attica, the tyrannical king compelled Athens to pay a tribute of seven youths and seven maidens every nine years, who were thrust one by one into the labyrinth to be pursued and destroyed in its winding passages, and bewildering exits, by the terrible Minotaur.

It is a favorite Greek hero tale of how Theseus, the heroic son of old King Aegeus of Attica, had himself appointed as one of the seven youths that he might fight the Minotaur. With his companions, he made the voyage to Crete and boldly confronted the iron-breasted king in his palace at Knossos, who promptly threw them into a dungeon with orders that Theseus be the first victim of the Minotaur before daybreak the following morning. But gentle Ariadne, the tender-hearted daughter of Minos, was so touched by the impending fate of these Athenian youths and maidens and was so impressed with the spirit of Prince Theseus, bearing himself so calmly in his terrible peril, that she resolved to save them from their awful fate. At midnight she awakened Theseus and took him forth from the darksome prison into the pleasant moonlight. She restored to him his gold-hilted sword and leading him gently by the hand, while she held a torch in her other hand, she brought him to the wall of the labyrinth, where a marble stone yielded to her touch and swung back for them to make entrance.

From this point on, we shall give the story in the words of Nathaniel Hawthorne, who has given the most interesting account of this incident to be found in American literature, in his beloved *Tanglewood Tales:*

> "We are now," said Ariadne, "in the famous labyrinth which Daedalus built before he made himself a pair of wings, and flew away from our island like a bird. That Daedalus was a very cunning

workman; but of all his artful contrivances, this labyrinth is the most wondrous. Were we to take but a few steps from the doorway, we might wander about all our lifetime, and never find it again. Yet in the very centre of this labyrinth is the Minotaur; and, Theseus, you must go thither to seek him."

"But how shall I ever find him," asked Theseus, "if the labyrinth so bewilders me as you say it will?"

Just as he spoke they heard a rough and very disagreeable roar, which greatly resembled the lowing of a fierce bull, but yet had some sort of sound like the human voice. Theseus even fancied a rude articulation in it, as if the creature that uttered it were trying to shape his hoarse breath into words. It was at some distance, however, and he really could not tell whether it sounded most like a bull's roar or a man's harsh voice.

"That is the Minotaur's voice," whispered Ariadne, closely grasping the hand of Theseus, and pressing one of her own hands to her heart, which was all in a tremble. "You must follow that sound through the windings of the labyrinth, and, by and by, you will find him. Stay! take the end of this silken string; I will hold the other end; and then, if you win the victory, it will lead you again to this spot. Farewell, brave Theseus."

So the young man took the end of the silken string in his left hand, and his gold-hilted sword, ready drawn from its scabbard, in the other, and trod boldly into the inscrutable labyrinth. How this labyrinth was built is more than I can tell you. But so cunningly contrived a mizmaze was never seen in the world, before nor since. There can be nothing else so intricate, unless it were the brain of a man like Daedalus, who planned it, or the heart of any ordinary man; which last, to be sure, is ten times as great a mystery as the labyrinth of Crete. Theseus had not taken five steps before he lost sight of Ariadne; and in five more his head was growing dizzy. But still he went on, now creeping through a low arch, now ascending a flight of steps, now in one crooked passage, and now in another, with here a door opening before him, and there one banging behind, until it really seemed as if the walls spun around, and whirled him round along with them.

As he passed onward, the clouds gathered over the moon, and the labyrinth grew so dusky that Theseus could no longer discern the bewilderment through which he was passing. He would have felt quite lost, and utterly hopeless of ever again walking in a straight path, if, every little while, he had not been conscious of a gentle twitch at the silken cord. Then he knew that the tender hearted Ariadne was still holding the other end, and that she was fearing for him, and hoping for him, and giving him just as much sympathy as if she were close by his side. O, indeed, I can assure you, there was a vast deal of human sympathy running along that slender thread of silk. But still he followed the dreadful roar of the Minotaur, which now grew louder and louder, and finally so very loud that Theseus fully expected to come close upon him, at every new zigzag and wriggle of the path. And at last, in an open space, at the very centre of the labyrinth, he did discern the hideous creature.

Then some very gusty repartee took place between the monster and the hero. The Minotaur lowered his horribly sharp horns, and Theseus brandished his shining sword, after which they "fell to" as Hawthorne narrates:

> Without more words on either side, there ensued the most awful fight between Theseus and the Minotaur that ever happened beneath the sun or moon. I really know not how it might have turned out, if the monster, in his first headlong rush against Theseus, had not missed him, by a hair's-breadth, and broken one of his horns short off against the stone wall. On this mishap, he bellowed so intolerably that a part of the labyrinth tumbled down, and all the inhabitants of Crete mistook the noise for an uncommonly heavy thunder storm. Smarting with the pain, he galloped around the open space in so ridiculous a way that Theseus laughed at it, long afterwards, though not precisely at the moment. After this, the antagonists stood valiantly up to one another, and fought sword to horn, for a long while. At last, the Minotaur made a run at Theseus, grazed his left side with his horn, and flung him down; and thinking that he had stabbed him to the heart, he cut a great caper in the air, opened his bull mouth from ear to ear, and prepared to snap his head off. But Theseus by this time had leaped up, and caught the monster off his guard. Fetching a sword stroke at him with all his force, he hit him fair upon the neck, and made his bull head skip six yards from his human body, which fell down flat upon the ground.

> So now the battle was ended. Immediately the moon shone out as brightly as if all the troubles of the world, and all the wickedness and the ugliness that infest human life, were past and gone forever. And Theseus, as he leaned on his sword, taking breath, felt another twitch of the silken cord; for all through the terrible encounter, he had held it fast in his left hand. Eager to let Ariadne know of his success, he followed the guidance of the thread, and soon found himself at the entrance of the labyrinth.

Taking gentle Ariadne with them, the grateful youths and maidens returned to Athens, making a real joy ride of the journey, after stopping for many delightful days on some of the pleasant isles, especially Naxos and Delos. Ariadne was left sleeping on the Island of Naxos where she later married the God Bacchus. Theseus became king of Attica soon after his return home and was of course a great legendary monarch.

THE EGYPTIAN LABYRINTH

A NTEDATING the mythical Cretan Labyrinth, there was a mighty architectural phenomenon in the north of Egypt known as The Egyptian Labyrinth. It is fairly well established that it must have been constructed as early as 2000 B. C. There is a record of this labyrinth that is genuinely historical. Indeed, it was written by Herodotus himself, the Father of History, who visited the spot in person about the middle of the Fifth Century B. C. and made a thorough study of its ruins as he found it at that time.

He wrote of it:

> I found it greater than words could tell, for although the temple at Ephesus and that at Samos are celebrated works, yet all of the works and buildings of the Greeks put together would certainly be inferior to this labyrinth as regards labour and expense. It has twelve covered courts, with opposite doors, six courts on the North side and six on the South, all communicating with one another and with one wall surrounding them all. There are two sorts of rooms, one sort above, the other sort below ground, fifteen hundred of each sort, or three thousand in all.

It was his opinion that this labyrinth in its original glory surpassed even the pyramids both in magnitude and significance. His research, however, was somewhat limited by the fact that he was permitted to go through only the upper rooms. The lower part, which was probably the most pretentious, was guarded from visitors. It contained the tombs of the twelve kings who were the builders of the labyrinth. It also contained the tombs of some sacred crocodiles which invested it with a religious significance peculiar to Egyptian life at that time. All vestiges of this monumental structure have since disappeared almost entirely. Such authentic records as are available, however, show that it was identified deeply with the spirit of a distinctive civilization.

THE BOWER OF ROSAMOND

OF less historic authenticity than the Egyptian Labyrinth was the mazy bower of fair Rosamond, which sustains a romantic interest in English literature and folklore equal to that of the Cretan Labyrinth. The legend in which this labyrinth, or maze, survives is enriched by the fact that it involves some well known characters of great English history. Consequently, it has been kept alive in English romance and literature for more than eight centuries.

The plot of the legend, of which the mazy bower of Rosamond was the principal stage, was laid in the reign of King Henry II, whose life span was from 1133 to 1189 A. D. His reign was one of the stormiest periods of English history, involving much romance and intrigue. Concerning King Henry, the romantic monarch of many illicit amours, the legend maintains that he designed a complicated maze, or labyrinth, in his park at Woodstock, as a convenient retreat for his romantic pastimes. His favorite paramour, according to historic gossip, was the lovely Rosamond. She is invested with a bit of historic reality. The persistent rumor prevails that she was the daughter of one of the king's most powerful knights, Sir Walter DeClifford. This, however, has never been fully verified.

According to the legend, this royal romance became involved in melancholy and tragedy because of the jealousy of the Queen, Eleanor of Aquitania. When she learned of this clandestine affair of her majestic spouse she was inspired with such regal jealousy that she contrived to solve the riddle of the labyrinth, or maze. Finding her way into its innermost recess, she confronted fair Rosamond and forced her to choose between a dagger and a bowl of poison. Rosamond chose the poison and thus came to her melancholy end.

This legend has provided a rich background for literary reflection both in poetry and prose. It has been preserved mainly in quaint ballads of some centuries past, such as the one which John Aubrey in his *Remaines,* written in 1686, tells us that his nurse often sang to him:

> Yea, Rosamond, Fair Rosamond,
>   Her name was called so,
> To whom dame Elinor our Queene
>   Was known a deadly foe,
> The King therefore for her defense
>   Aginst the furious Queene
> At Woodstock builded such a Bower
>   The like was never seen.

Most curiously that Bower was built
   Of stone and timber strong,
An hundred and fifty dores
   Did to this Bower belong,
And they so cunningly contriv'd
   With turnings round about
That none but with a clew of thread
   Could enter in or out.

HAMPTON COURT MAZE

PERHAPS the most notable English labyrinth, next to that of fair Rosamond, is the maze of Hampton Court, which flourishes yet today. It was constructed in 1690 in the days of William III, who is known in history as William of Orange. It bears suggestion of the continental background of this English monarch and was designed by his gardeners, George London and Henry Wise. It is believed to have displaced an older maze, a relic of the time of Cardinal Wolsey, situated close to the Bushy Park entrance of what was called the "Wilderness," a preserve that replaced an old orchard of the palace. Although today it bears the name of maze, it was spoken of in the lines of Defoe as a "labyrinth."

It was and is much less pretentious than the other great labyrinths of which we have made mention. It seems to reflect the well cultivated taste of William of Orange in its neat and symmetrical pattern, which contained sufficient puzzle to invest it with a mystic interest and to afford amusement. It is very modest in its proportions, occupying less than a half acre of ground. Its total length of pathway is about half a mile and its longest side measures 222 feet. It is a typical hedge labyrinth and was first composed entirely of hornbeam. Having required frequent renewals in various parts through the centuries, it has come to represent something of a patchwork of privet, hornbeam, yew, holly, hawthorn and sycamore. Instead of an inner temple, the goal that is reached after threading its winding passages, consists of two bench seats, each shaded by a leafy tree. Thus, it will be seen that this world famed maze is much less elaborate than the restored Labyrinth in New Harmony. However, it still retains a simple symmetry and has maintained its popularity to modern times, offering rare enjoyment to the hundreds of children together with many elders who visit it on summer holidays. The gate receipts have totaled as much as $4,000.00 in a single year.

Its symbolical meaning is suggested in the following lines, taken from the British Magazine for 1747, which were written as *Reflections that came from walking in the Maze at Hampton Court.*

> What is this mighty labyrinth—the earth,
> But a wild maze the moment of our birth?
> Still as we life pursue the maze extends,
> Nor find we where each winding purlieu ends;
> Crooked and vague each step of life we tread,—
> Unseen the danger, we escape the dread!

But with delight we through the labyrinth range,
Confused we turn, and view each artful change—
Bewildered, through each wild meander bend
Our wandering steps, anxious to gain the end;
Unknown and intricate, we still pursue
Like hoodwinked fools, perplex'd we grope our way
And during life's short course we blindly stray,
Puzzled in mazes and perplex'd with fears;
Unknown alike both heaven and earth appears.
Till at the last, to banish our surprise,
Grim death unbinds the napkin from our eyes.
Then shall Gay's truth and wisdom stand confest,
And *Death* will show us *Life* was but a jest.

HAMPTON COURT MAZE

(From Mathews *Mazes and Labyrinths* with permission of
Longmans, Green and Co., Publishers)

PRINCE OF ANHAULT LABYRINTH

BY well established German tradition a famous Prince of Anhault constructed a fantastic labyrinth in his palace garden. A very large composite creation, it was purely allegorical, portending to typify the inevitable course of human life. Although the body of the labyrinth proper was constructed principally of hedges, it also contained rocks, trees and even streams and caverns. Among these, tortuous paths were deeply cut. Some of the winding ways were partly covered so that a somber darkness was maintained throughout with barely enough illumination to light the way of the wanderer step by step. At well arranged intervals all along the way, there were various allegorical devices in the form of images and tablets. The tablets bore inscriptions. Both the imagery and inscriptions tended to augment reflection upon the mysterious and fearsome ways of life.

Some of these allegorical manifestations were said to have been fine examples of sculpture. The symbolical suggestions were not entirely somber. There were some refreshing oases in the form of flowery dells. These fragrant recesses, together with other pleasing devices of plant life, were suggestive of Elysium. All this lives only in tradition, which, however, is very well established in German folklore. If these traditions may be believed, that labyrinth of the Prince of Anhault was indeed a very elaborate design, including all the outstanding features that have characterized the best known labyrinths of the world.

CHURCH LABYRINTHS

INFORMATION is to be found in medieval literature of an extensive variety of Church labyrinths. They were quite common during the middle ages nearly everywhere throughout middle Europe. Not much history has been preserved as to any particular example but the same general character seems to have been exhibited in nearly all of them. They carried definite religious significance in their symbolism of the manifold perplexities and the disheartening intricacies that beset the Christian path. Some of them carried more alluring suggestions in concrete ways of the intriguing and entangling nature of sin. They pointed out in graphic symbols the darkness that certainly involved the wandering believer if he ventured on any deviation from the straight and narrow course of Christian duty.

Thus the Christian church gave to the labyrinth a much higher significance than it bore originally. As a design for ornamenting church robes, the labyrinth was indicative of the numerous and complicated folds of sin by which man is enveloped and from which he cannot be extricated except through the aid of Providence.

There is some basis for the belief that these labyrinths were made to serve a practical, as well as an allegorical purpose, by providing the setting for penitential pilgrimages. In the days of the early Crusades it was a common practice for stern father confessors to sentence peccant members of their flocks to enlistment in the Crusades or to take distant pilgrimages of various kinds. The favored pilgrimage of that day was a visit to the Holy Sepulchre, which in the time of the Crusades involved joining in the fight against the invading infidels.

With the decline of the valiant spirit of the Crusades, shorter and less dangerous pilgrimages were substituted in the way of mild adventures to be had in threading these mystic mazes. It has been maintained by some writers that penitents have been required to traverse pavement labyrinths on their knees—symbolizing the path from the house of Pilate to Calvary, over which Christ's journey took about two hours. Even before the Crusades had entirely ended, this form of penance was frequently imposed upon defaulting Christians, who from physical weakness or for some other compelling reason were unable to take the arduous journey to the Holy Land.

After the Church adopted the labyrinth, as symbolical of itself, the custom of building labyrinthian figures in cathedral floors of black and yellow tile began. These were used as instruments of performing penance for sins of commission and omission, especially the nonfulfill-ment of vows. Symbolizing pilgrimages to the Holy Land, they were called "Chemins de Jerusalem." Two thousand steps had to be taken to reach the center after the right path had been chosen; but the pilgrim was first allured by devious and winding ways which led him in wrong directions. In the center, to which the path eventually led him, figures of bishops and saints were placed, ranging around a central cross. This signified that they rested in the bosom of the Church.

Such spiritual labyrinths of allegorical design were generally in vogue in Europe until the last quarter of the 18th century. The latest known to be built was in Lyon, France, in 1769. There were no allegorical labyrinths in the churches of England. The idea of the labyrinth was taken there by the invading Roman army, where it was given a new form of interpretation in the turf maze.

Turf mazes of intricate and winding design, which stood out in bold relief as the surrounding turf was cut away, existed only in England. Illustrations are to be found of figures of nuns and devout women winding their way through the maze upon their knees telling their beads. These turf formations were sometimes alluded to as Troy Towns, or as Julian's Bower. Julian, (or Julus), son of Aeneas, was credited with having brought the first maze to Italy.

The labyrinths of medieval Europe, all of which had some church association, may be classified generally in three types—floors of cathe-drals, turf mazes on lawns in England, and clipped hedges, formed into circuitous paths. These hedge labyrinths, or mazes, were formed by planting yew, holly, and hornbean forming a design by which the cor-rect path led to a center that typified the Holy City—Jerusalem. Only the hedge labyrinths had a structure in the center which was variously known as a garden house, or temple. It was a place in which the pilgrim could contemplate the complicated folds of sin by which man was surrounded and from which there was no escape, except through the guiding hand of providence—similar to the symbolism of labyrinthine Church robes.

The placing of statues, vases, seats, fountains, and other ornaments at various points along the winding path was a later development, for the purpose of relieving the monotony of the walks. This practice attained its highest point during the 17th century in the labyrinth of a small park at Versailles, France. It contained some sightly sun dials with mottoes that were popular in the days of Louis XIV.

During the reigns of Henry VIII and his daughter, Elizabeth, the maze was quite popular throughout England. Practically all of these have been destroyed, altogether or·in part, and are only to be remembered by the survival of the tradition and the word maze in the various vicinities where they were planted. Out of all this a simplified garden maze gradually developed from which grew the modern design of dignity and beauty of garden flora as we now know it.

A pious chart, signed "Belion Fecit," was printed at Lyons in 1769, which is quite illuminating as to the fundamental conception of Church labyrinths. It was about this time that some fine cathedral labyrinths were being destroyed in France. The chart was intended to depict some definite spiritual suggestions derived from them. A part of the inscription reads as follows:

> The spiritual labyrinth ornamented with four channels of grace representing
> (a) the four rivers of the Earthly Paradise and the happy state of Man before the Fall;
> (b) by divers convolutions, the various miseries with which human life has since been beset;
> (c) by the fact of the labyrinth terminating at the same point as that from which it starts, we see how Man, being formed of earth, returns, as to his first principle, by the decay of the body;
> (d) the health-giving waters of these channels represent the grace of God in which the depraved soul finds its remedy.

ETRUSCAN LABYRINTHS

WE learn from Pliny that in his day (first century A. D.) there were some noted Etruscan labyrinths. According to his expressions concerning them they seem to have partaken, for the most part, of a purely sepulchral character. Such miscellaneous descriptions as were given them indicate that they bore some similarity to the catacombs of Rome, Paris, and Naples. The principal feature of such a labyrinth was a long, winding, somber path following a very intricate pattern, with graves and tombs and other sepulchral signs appearing along the way. This was their usual character. However, they were not always correlated with sepulchral sentiments, as the word "labyrinth" in its application to them seemed to imply that some of these constructions embodied merely an intricate way without any special allegorical implication.

It will be noted in this connection that the character of the tomb was also a major feature of the great Egyptian labyrinth. However, it served the purpose of a tomb only for certain kings and for the sacred crocodiles; whereas the Etruscan labyrinth seemed to serve the purpose of entombment generally. It is not to be understood, however, that they were merely cemeteries. They were intended rather to suggest death and the grave in an allegorical sense rather than to serve as burial places.

It seems that nowhere at any time have labyrinths departed from their main character of exhibitng symbolism rather than of serving concrete uses.

THE LABYRINTH IN LITERATURE

A S already observed the labyrinth, or maze, has been for centuries a
subject for passing comment in the literature of many languages
and has been made the setting of some noted plots in fiction. The
words themselves have had varied adaptations as different parts of
speech. Always, the labyrinth has maintained its elusive and mystical
character in all of its widely diversified literary applications.

Samuel Johnson said in his *Works*:

> To tell of disappointment and misery, to thicken the darkness of
> futurity, and perplex the labyrinth of uncertainty, has always been a
> delicious employment of the poets.

Cowper in *The Task* declares:

> . . . Some the style
> Infatuates, and through labyrinths and wilds
> Of error leads them by a tune entranc'd.

Milton explains that:

> The ingenuous reader, without further amusing himself in the
> labyrinth of controversial antiquity, may come the speediest way to
> see the truth vindicated.

And Fuller admonishes:

> An index is a necessary implement . . . without this, a large
> author is but a labyrinth without a clew to direct the readers within!

Thomas Jefferson wrote the following comment with special reference
to politics and diplomacy:

> Though you cannot see when you take one step what will be the
> next, yet follow truth, justice, and plain dealing, and never fear their
> leading you out of the labyrinth.

Shakespeare makes frequent use of both labyrinth and maze. For
instance, in his *Midsummer Night's Dream* he had Titania say, in her
reply to Oberon after he had twitted her about her love for Theseus:

> . . . the quaint mazes in the wanton green,
> For lack of threading are undistinguishable.

THE LABYRINTH

In *The Tempest* he makes Gonzalo, the old counsellor, exclaim:

> By'r lakin, I can go no further, sir,
> My old bones ache; here's a maze trod indeed
> Through forth rights and meanders: by your patience
> I needs must rest me.

In this same play Alonzo asserts:

> This is as strange a maze as e'er man trod:
> And there is in this business more than nature
> Was ever conduct of.

In *King Henry VI*, the Earl of Suffolk exclaims concerning Margaret of Aujou whose hand he had been soliciting for the king:

> O, wert thou for myself:—But, Suffolk, stay;
> Thou mayst not wander in that labyrinth;
> There Minotaur and ugly treason lurk.

Petruchio declares in *The Taming of the Shrew*:

> I have thrust myself into this maze
> Haply to wive and thrive as best I may.

In the tragedy of *Troilus and Cressida*, Thersites bursts forth in dramatic soliloquy before the tent of Achilles with this exclamation:

> Here no, Thersites! What, lost in this
> labyrinth of thy fury?

These lines from an old ballad seem to apply to a game, recalling with clear suggestion the myth of the Cretan Labyrinth:

> Beware the dreadful Minotaur
> That dwells within the Maze.
> The monster feasts on human gore
> And bones of those he slays;
> Then softly through the labyrinth creep
> And rouse him not to strife.
> Take one short peep, prepare to leap
> And run to save your life!

Francis Thompson begins his poem, *The Hound of Heaven*, as follows:

> I fled Him, down the nights and down the days;
> I fled Him, down the arches of the years;
> I fled Him, down the labyrinthine ways
> Of my own mind; . . .

IN HISTORY, MYTHOLOGY, LITERATURE, AND ART

The following excerpts taken somewhat at random illustrate the wide range of usage of labyrinth and maze:

Lethe, the River of Oblivion, rolls
Her wat'ry labyrinth, whereof who drinks
Forthwith his former state and being forgets.
>—*Milton, Paradise Lost.*

Yet in the maddening maze of things,
And tossed by storm and flood
To one fixed trust my spirit clings
I know that God is good.
>—*Whittier, The Eternal Goodness.*

He cranks and crosses with a thousand doubles;
The many musets through the which he goes
Are like a labyrinth to amaze his foes.
>—*Shakespeare, Venus and Adonis.*

No thread is left else
To guide us from this labyrinth of mischief.
>—*Fletcher, Double Marriage.*

Whereby men wander in the dark, and
in labyrinths of errour.
>—*Purchas, Pilgrimage.*

Alike all ages; dames of ancient days
Have led their children through the mirthful maze;
>—*Goldsmith, The Traveller.*

As through the verdant maze
Of sweetbrier hedges I pursue my walk;
Or taste the smell of dairy.
>—*Thomson, The Seasons—Spring.*

But while listening Senates hang upon thy tongue,
Devolving through the maze of eloquence
A roll of periods sweeter than her song.
>—*Thomson, The Seasons—Autumn.*

Within a bony labyrinthean cave
Reached by the pulse of the aerial wave,
This sibyl, sweet, and Mystic Sense is found,
Muse, that presides o'er all the Powers of Sound.
>—*Abraham Coles, Man the Microcosm;*
>*and the Cosmos.*

Some are bewilder'd in the maze of schools,
And some made coxcombs Nature meant but fools.
>—*Pope, Essay on Criticism.*

Expatiate free o'er all this scene of man;
A mighty maze! but not without a plan.
>—*Pope, Essay on Man.*

THE LABYRINTH

Let no maze intrude
Upon your spirits.
—Marston and Webster, Malcontent.

To pry into the maze of his counsels is not only folly
in man, but presumption even in angels.
—Sir T. Browne, Religio Medici.

They lose themselves in the very maze of their
own discourses.
—Hooker, Eccles. Polity.

From Helicon's harmonious springs
A thousand rills their mazy progress take.
—Thomas Gray, The Progress of Posey.

In all the mazes of metaphysical confusion.
—Junius, Letters.

The melting voice in mazes running.
—Milton, L'Allegro.

Mark how the labyrinthian turns they take,
The circles intricate, and mystic maze.
—Young, Night Thoughts.

To entangle, trammel up, and snare
Your sense in wine and labyrinth you there.
—Keats, Lamia.

Such illustrations can be multiplied indefinitely. They serve to show the wide range of sentiment attaching to the words "labyrinth" and "maze." It is clear that they are almost perfectly interchangeable in adaptation. Always they are made to carry the implication of something mysteriously complicated.

These words are often used in titles of books, plays and poems, such as:

Stewart:	THE MAZE
Gilchrist:	THE LABYRINTH
Wood:	WITHIN THE MAZE
Tiddy:	THE MAZE OF SICILY
Shirley:	LOVE IN A MAZE
Fletcher:	A LOVER'S MAZE
Scott:	THE PHYSIOLOGY OF THE HUMAN LABYRINTH

THE LABYRINTH IN ART

MAZES and labyrinths have had extensive recognition in various forms of art, especially on badges and official decorations. Here again, in the same way as in literature, it is the symbolism attaching to them that is given significance. One of the most characteristic applications of this idea is found in the practice of some early Roman emperors of having the figure of the labyrinth woven artistically in many colors on their imperial robes.

An old manuscript suggests the allegorical lesson that was taught through this symbolism in the following legend:

> Let there be represented on it (The Emperor's robe) a labyrinth of gold and pearls, in which the Minotaur, made of emerald, holds his finger to his mouth, thus signifying that, just as none may know the secret of the labyrinth, so none may reveal the monarch's counsels.

So again we see the element of mystery symbolized as the primary suggestion of the labyrinth.

LABYRINTHINE EXERCISES

THE labyrinth naturally lends itself to a wide range of games, dances, and various forms of pageantry. Its winding lanes encourage children's games and races within the labyrinth itself. In a symbolical way it suggests more elaborate games and exercises that may well be conducted around it. Consequently, it is fortunate that our restored Labyrinth offers an inviting plaza or esplanade in the foreground, well suited to such exercises and to such pageantry as may be desired, in connection with pilgrimages to the Labyrinth.

There is a very unique historical background for labyrinthine dances. When Theseus and his youthful companions returned in triumph after their rescue from the Minotaur in the Cretan Labyrinth, they stopped for an extended period of several weeks on the inviting Island of Delos. While there, they fabricated a mysterious dance which was based upon the mysticism of the labyrinth. It consisted of winding formations and dazzling turns, symbolical of the threading of the labyrinth with its many hidden ways, distracting divagations, and dead ends.

This dance was perpetuated by the natives of Delos. It became known as the Geranos, or Crane Dance, and survived for many centuries. It was probably the origin of the custom that has been followed in many other countries of practicing mystical dances and rhythmical games, suggesting the sinuous windings of the labyrinth.

For example, Virgil described the complicated movements of such a dance involving the convolutions of the Cretan Labyrinth as follows:

> As when in lofty Crete (so fame reports)
> The Labyrinth of old, in winding walls
> A mazy way inclos'd a thousand paths
> Ambiguous and perplexed, by which the steps
> Should by an error intricate, untrac'd
> Be still deluded.

There is still practiced even today in France a children's game called Labyrinthe, in which most of the players form a chain of arches by holding hands, while two runners known as the "weaver" and the "shuttle" thread with agile dance the arches so formed.

It is very fitting therefore that the encouragement of all such appropriate exercises at the restored New Harmony Labyrinth should be made a definite feature of the Memorial, so that the conduct of suitable games within the Labyrinth and on the foreground around the big elm tree should be established as a regular custom in connection with the visitation of organized groups, especially school groups. This custom was inaugurated at the Labyrinth on April 22, 1940, when Professor George E. Schlafer, Assistant Professor of Physical Education at Indiana University, started the training of the entire New Harmony High School, 110 boys and girls with their teachers, in the rendition of some rhythmical games and dances that he had adapted for this purpose. He conducted these original exercises in person and left specific designs and directions.

These directions are placed in the hands of teachers of physical education in all schools contemplating pilgrimages to New Harmony, so that with a little preliminary training they can play the games at the Labyrinth before they thread its winding ways. Such games furnish enlivening exercise and tend to inculcate in the students, both physically and mentally, a true spirit introduction to the significance of the Labyrinth. Such purposeful activities reflect the very highest form of applied psychology. Naturally the development of these exercises will gradually lead to the rendition of simple pageantry of all kinds around the old elm tree.

Thus, at our restored New Harmony Labyrinth, young people of modern times can commend to themselves all the mythological inspiration that may come from the classic legend of the heroic Theseus and his companions in their journey to and from the Labyrinth of Crete. They may also exercise their ingenuity and resourcefulness in games and races within the winding ways of the Labyrinth.

Incidentally, it is worthy of special note in this connection that the maze is used extensively in modern psychology as a graphic object for mental testing, especially of children.

A LABYRINTHINE DANCE

PART III

Ufye Buuilders of tfye Labyrintf

RELIGION AND MYSTICISM OF THE
HARMONY SOCIETY

THERE can be no doubt that the Labyrinth built by the Harmonists had intimate relation with their religion and perhaps even more with what might be called their mysticism. This is not easy to explain. They left no positive records concerning it. Nevertheless, the subject admits of thoughtful inquiry into the religion they professed so sincerely and into the mysticism which was strangely, though naturally, involved in their spiritual conceptions. That the construction and use of the Labyrinth was involved symbolically in all this must be accepted, even though the exact relationship is not easily determined. In any case this treatise is the fitting place in which to set forth the main religious tenets and practices of those pious founders of Harmonie, who were the builders of the Labyrinth. Out of this the thoughtful reader may draw his own conclusions as to the proper association of Harmonist life with the Labyrinth and with the history of labyrinths generally.

The Harmony Society exhibited a high type of religious socialization. Though it should not be designated technically as a religious society, in an orthodox sense, yet it is certainly true that religion was its most controlling factor. Religious influences and religious teachings entered into every phase of the lives of these pious people. Definite forms of religious worship constituted a regular and important part of their activities. Work and worship occupied nearly all of their time and effort, and the two activities were most intimately integrated. It is no undue extension of plain facts to say that the Harmony Society both in its idealistic conceptions and in the actual contemplation of all the members—certainly of the leaders—tried to maintain upon earth an annex to the Kingdom of Heaven.

Fortunately during their sojourn here a quaint little book was pro-duced—written, printed, and published here—that may be taken as the authentic expression of the religious basis of the Harmony Society. This book, of which only a few copies now remain, is entitled *Thoughts on the Destiny of Man, Particularly with Reference to the Present Times by The Harmony Society in Indiana, A. D. 1824.* It was written by Father Rapp himself, assisted perhaps by the learned school master, Dr. Muller. Select quotations from it as the best expression of their creed will be included in this brief treatise.

In its characterization of the Harmony Society, this booklet says unqualifiedly that:

> A harmonious and united society of men may be said to be a King-dom of God.

It explains further:

> True Christians are united to each other, by a solemn covenant of friendship and brotherly love, and thus form a Kingdom of Heaven upon Earth, where all their spiritual and temporal interests are closely connected together, and where the purest benevolence influences every one, to the greatest exertion, for the welfare of the Whole.

Thus was expressed the close union of spiritual and temporal interests which the Harmony Society exemplified to a very remarkable degree. It would be difficult to find anywhere in history a more striking combina-tion of practicality and mysticism. They actually sought to make the Kingdom of God a "genuine reality."

> Whoever imagines the Kingdom of God too spiritual, errs in head and heart. Every spirit in its progressive development seeks symmetry, equilibrium, and proportion, with its bodily substance, that it may be enabled to express itself, and act physically, in the human sense.

Upon this conception a practical brotherhood was established, the Harmony Society, which carried on regularly in the following manner:

> In the common household of this BROTHERHOOD, the greatest order, diligence, and skill, are observed in the most minute, as well as in the most extensive transaction. Here wealth is possessed in abundance, and all cares for sustenance are removed and forgotten. No sluggard can live in this amicable confederation, for permission is never given to any one to eat his bread in sinful indolence. Male and female, old and young, are usefully employed, according to their powers of mind and body; all contribute to the WELFARE OF THE WHOLE, and from the common stock, every individual is supplied with all the necessaries of life.

Out of all this, they were privileged to enjoy prosperity and complete economic security.

> Here are possessed sufficient means for convenience, and a competent knowledge for their application, to the rational and useful purposes of life. Where so many useful, active powers, are harmoniously united, there must be, and evidently is, a true Kingdom of God.

The practical operation of their harmonious system is further elaborated in this paragraph:

> In this BROTHERHOOD is founded a system of social order, both in spiritual and temporal affairs, of civil policy, and of ecclesiastical discipline, where the precepts of religion, and the principles of morality, pervade and regulate the whole; and where the rights of men are carefully secured by a covenant of their own free will, their interests promoted by the united exertions of their ingenuity and industry, and their minds enlightened and refined, by the knowledge and practise of the divine doctrines of Jesus Christ, and of the political and moral lessons of human reason. Happy Society! An example to the rest of mankind of social concord and harmonious liberty!

So it was that in this spiritual and temporal union a most unusual harmony was realized. Never was a term more fittingly applied than the name Harmony for the Society and Harmonie for the town they founded. All their efforts were directed "by the fundamental rules of harmony." They considered their life here to be a natural progression. As their creed recites:

> There is no stopping nor retrograding in the Kingdom of Heaven, but a pressing forward to the goal where a temple of God is erected in a green and tranquil and delightful valley, that those who are susceptible of light may find consolation and repose, and worship in the holy Tabernacle, in unison, in order, and in harmony.

They made it work in the daily living relations of the members with each other.

> Here, the members kindly assist each other, in difficulty and danger and share with each other the enjoyments and the misfortunes of life; one lives in the breast of another, and forgets himself; all their undertakings are influenced by a social spirit; glowing with noble energy and generous feeling, and pressing forward to the haven of their mutual prosperity.

They justified these idealistic principles economically, as they truthfully asserted:

> Nothing can be compared to a religious society, that succeeds in properly uniting its temporal with its spiritual concerns. It can do everything. That which a single individual in a long time and at an enormous expense can scarcely or perhaps not at all accomplish, is achieved by such a society in a short time and with but very trifling cost.

Their religious socialization might have been based specifically upon Acts IV:32:

> And the multitude of them that believed were of one heart and one
> soul; neither said any of them that aught of the things which he pos-
> sessed was his own; but they had all things, common.

They conformed to this doctrine in every particular. All their
wealth was put into a common fund. Although at first it was provided
that in case of the withdrawal of any member his money should be
refunded to him without interest or that he should be awarded such
a sum as his conduct justified in case he had come in without capital,
this provision was later abrogated. And in 1818 all records of any
kind evidencing individual property were destroyed and they bound
themselves unqualifiedly to the resolution:

> We endure and suffer, labor and toil, sow and reap, with and for
> each other.

There was scriptural background for everything they did, which was
authoritatively expressed in the preamble to their Articles of Association: (1827)

> WHEREAS, By the favor of Divine Providence, an association, or
> community, has been formed by George Rapp and many others, upon
> the basis of Christian Fellowship, the principles of which being faith-
> fully derived from the sacred Scriptures, include the government of the
> patriarchal age, united to the community of property adopted in the
> days of the apostles, and wherein, the single object sought is to
> approximate, so far as human imperfection may allow, to the fulfill-
> ment of the will of God, by the exercise of those affections, and the
> practice of those virtues which are essential to the happiness of man
> in time and throughout eternity—

By their united observance of these principles in daily work they
achieved unparalleled prosperity. There was no loss of time or effort,
no waste of any kind. Harmony was exemplified in every phase of
their life. They were universally law-abiding. They really made of
Harmonie—

> A Noble Asylum! where brethren live together in unity and love, and
> form upon earth, a Kingdom of God.

Thus they qualified themselves—

> for the pure enjoyments of that brotherly union, where the true prin-
> ciples of religion and the prudent regulations of industry and economy,
> by their united influence, produce a *heaven upon earth—a true*
> HARMONY.

This extraordinary mode of living and its fundamental basis must
be taken into consideration in arriving at any true understanding of

the history of the founders of old Harmonie on the Wabash and in the memorialization of the great symbols they left here. The Labyrinth was a part of all this. It certainly exemplified in an idealistic way the extension of their spiritual conceptions into the realm of lofty mysticism. And it admonished them pleasantly of the safety of the harmony way of life compared with the dangerous paths by which one may "become lost and bewildered in the labyrinth of the artificial philosophy of the world."

FATHER GEORGE RAPP

(1757-1847)

IT goes without saying that the Labyrinth of the Harmony Society was probably the creation of Father George Rapp. It was perhaps the most concrete expression of his strange mysticism. In this remarkable individual were combined the extremes of spirituality and common sense—practicality and mysticism. It is generally understood that in him and through him is to be found the best exemplification of the spiritual significance of the Harmony Society.

He was the patriarch, preacher, and prophet of the Society. Indeed, he was its original founder and certainly he was the main controlling factor of that association in all its stages for more than half a century. The Society functioned legally as "George Rapp and Associates." It should be explained here that the members of this Society did not call themselves Rappites. They were Harmonists or Harmonians. But history has justly and irrevocably characterized them as Rappites because of the preeminence of Father Rapp and his great foster son, Frederick Rapp.

In 1787, when George Rapp was thirty years of age, he began preaching what might be called a Separatist form of socialized religion in the little town of Eptingen, in the Province of Wurttemberg, Germany. He was by occupation a weaver and vine dresser. Although he was not highly educated, he became a profound student of the Scriptures, and he expounded his new doctrine with such effect that he developed a following in that community, which gradually solidified into what might be called a homogeneous brotherhood.

It was out of his teaching and preaching that the prevailing tenets of the Rappite faith were developed. Some of his views were most extreme. For example, he professed belief in the biunity of man. It may have been partly because of this profession that the doctrine of celibacy finally became prevalent in the Harmony Society, although he does not seem to have been the first to suggest it. There is no doubt that he believed sincerely in the near approach of the millennium. He never doubted that the world would come to an end in his day and that he would be vouchsafed the privilege of presenting all his followers ready for the ascension at the second coming of Christ.

A born leader, six feet tall and of powerful physique, he had the commanding stature and bearing of one who spoke and acted with authority. Although his contemplation ranged far into the realm of idealism, he was intensely practical. As firmly as he believed in his spiritual creed, he also advocated and practiced the simple virtues of hard work and self-denial.

An authoritative statement of his unqualified preeminence in the Society is found in the history of the Harmony Society by Dr. Aaron Williams, which was approved in a written endorsement on September 1, 1866, by R. L. Baker and Jacob Henrici, the two trustees who succeeded Rapp. After reciting how he organized his followers and led them to America where the Harmony Society was formally founded February 15, 1805, Williams says:

> To give Rapp's subsequent personal history would be to give the history of the Society in detail for more than forty years. He was its civil and religious head, its prophet, priest, and king. He dictated all its rules and regulations, and was the supreme arbiter in all questions that arose. His word was law. It was enough to know that "Father Rapp says it," to satisfy all the community on any subject whatever. All this power, however, was administered, not selfishly or tyrannically, but in a truly patriarchal spirit, and with a single eye to the temporal and spiritual welfare of his people, who loved and reverenced him as a father, and never thought of questioning his right to all the authority which he claimed.

His almost absolute leadership was qualified by great kindness of heart. Although he was looked upon by the outside world as an autocrat, actually he ruled only by love and kindness. He had the confidence of his people, and he entered sincerely into all their concerns with the genuine regard of a loving father. Indeed, he was a patriarch as truly as Abraham of old was a patriarch. He guided and guarded his little flock as a faithful shepherd. He even maintained an informal confessional through which he preserved individual harmony among his followers. No appeal was ever made to him in vain. He settled all individual difficulties and troubles daily and thus put into effect his rule of community harmony—"Let not the sun go down upon your wrath." He tried to see to it that when the lights went out at the ringing of the curfew, the troubled souls of the little community had been relieved of all disturbances and were prepared to sleep in harmony.

He preached regularly twice on Sundays and sometimes during the week. His ruling doctrine was: "Love to God above all and to thy neighbor as thyself." Whether or not he actually used any special devices to strengthen his leadership, such as signs, tokens, symbols and secret passages, cannot be historically asserted. Certainly, he professed to receive divine intimations in dreams and visions. It is generally accepted that the large brick church, built in the form of a Maltese Cross, was the result of a definite vision, which came to him several different times. The Duke of Saxe-Weimar made the following note of this in his journal on the occasion of his visit to New Harmony in 1826:

> Rapp, they say, had dreamed three times that this building should be erected, and therefore he had it done.

There is further contemporary confirmation of this in the stately greeting which he received from Frankfort-on-the-Main, July 14, 1829, heralding the coming of Count de Leon. It contained this sentence:

> It was an omen or token from God, that you should build a church in the form of a cross, in accordance with a vision in sleep, and that you chose the "golden rose" for the symbol, according to the prophet Micha; for this golden rose shall in truth come to you.

It is probable that he maintained a secret passage from the basement of his house to the fort granary, where the silver treasure of the Society was kept, and it is possible also that he had a similar passage to the great church. He walked and talked among his people constantly, taking a direct interest in all their doings. He was very seldom away from the community, except on the three notable occasions when he went ahead with a vanguard to start each of the three separate settle-ments of the Society—Harmonie, Pennsylvania, in 1804; Harmonie, Indiana, in 1814; and Economy, Pennsylvania, in 1824. He controlled all agricultural operations and sometimes worked in the fields. It was said that "he could perform the greatest labor without fatigue, for his was a marvelous constitution."

It is certain that he frequently exhorted his people at their labors in the fields from high points on the hillside through a trumpet, an odd sort of metal megaphone, which is now preserved in the New Harmony Library and Museum. The famous "seat" of Father Rapp on the summit of a picturesque hill just outside of Harmony, Penn-sylvania, is indeed a "high" point of Harmonist interest. It consists of a flat ledge of rock upon which one may sit in ease and safety with the feet resting upon a similar ledge just beneath it. The commanding view of the entire valley that may be had from this "seat" is worth the hazardous climb up the almost perpendicular cliff from the nearest point on the roadside below.

His home was built in the heart of the little town of Harmonie on the Wabash at the very spot where his vanguard of one hundred men spent that first night in June, 1814—right there where under a huge oak tree, they first poured forth their fervent prayers and their lusty songs of hope and cheer. It was a "square mansion of brick," described by an English traveller as "very large and handsome, and would be esteemed a good house in any part of Europe." Unfortunately, it was burned in 1844. The stately Corbin home, known as the Rapp-Maclure Place, was built upon its foundations.

The Rapp home was ever a place of welcome and hospitality "for the honor of the society." It was the home of Father Rapp and his wife, Christina, their daughter, Rosina, their daughter-in-law, Johana, and her daughter, Gertrude. Frederick Rapp also lived there with them. Both in Harmonie and Economy, Pennsylvania, Frederick had a separate house.

Father Rapp was a lover of flowers and was an authority upon this species of horticulture, maintaining an extensive green house and garden plantation in his own yard. He was a constant student of history, literature, and various sciences, as well as the Bible. It cannot be doubted that he knew much of the history and literature concerning ancient and medieval labyrinths. It was natural that the symbolism of the labyrinth should appeal to him and that upon this symbol he had the Labyrinth constructed in Harmonie. There is no record as to just what use was made of it in connection with his ministrations among his people. The realm of fancy may well include the possibility that he used it as a means both of penance and reward.

The impression was current among visitors that it was used largely as a pleasure ground. Whatever its purpose and use, it must be con-cluded that it was in harmony with the purposes of Father Rapp. He was the spiritual leader of his followers up to the very hour of his death, at the age of 90 in 1847. After the death of his adopted son, Frederick Rapp in 1834, he was also the temporal head of the Society. During his long career of responsible leadership, he maintained all his prevailing views with absolute fidelity. He was a mystic through-out life, as well as a most sincere and practical Christian.

Father Rapp is at rest in the plain old cemetery at Economy. He lies in a moundless, unmarked grave among his faithful followers. A large bush grows near it by which the spot may be pointed out. There is an interesting episode connected with this spot, indicative of the fact that Father Rapp lived on not only in the hearts of Harmonists generally, but also in the very souls of leaders who succeeded him.

Most outstanding among these was Jacob Henrici, who was appointed one of the two governing trustees upon the demise of Father Rapp and later became the supreme head of the Society. From 1868 until his death in 1892, he stood in the shoes of Father Rapp, of whom he was ever a most devoted disciple. He is generally known in history as Father Henrici; but to the Harmonists of his day, he was Jacob. George Rapp was the only "Father" of the Harmony Society.

When Jacob first became the preacher of the Society, his sermons did not suit the congregation. He was too forthright and outspoken. "He called a spade a spade and a dung hook a dung hook." The Society took him to task about it and called a meeting to discipline him—perhaps to choose another preacher. But Jacob did not attend the meeting. A scarching party found him in the cemetery, lying on the grave of Father Rapp.

FATHER RAPP

FREDERICK RAPP

(1775-1834)

IT is likely that the physical design of the Labyrinth was drawn by Frederick Rapp, adopted son of Father Rapp. His real name was Frederick Reichert. Pursuit of his trade of stone cutter and architect had brought him, as a wide awake young man, into the neighborhood where George Rapp was preaching. His heart was touched by Rapp's words and he "soon became a devoted adherent and a member of Rapp's family."

He became the material genius and the temporal head of the Harmony Society. As a practical architect and engineer, he attended to the physical planning and building for the entire community. In this capacity he no doubt laid out the lines for the planting of the hedge rows that formed the Labyrinth. He may have helped choose the materials in the form of flowering shrubs and trees of which the hedge rows were constructed, and, of course, he designed the inner temple of the Labyrinth.

All this was no doubt done under the direct inspiration of Father Rapp, although it is quite possible that Frederick entered as heartily into the mystic contemplation of the Labyrinth as Father Rapp, for he was also mystically inclined and was devoted to art, music and poetry. As a cultured and learned man, he was familiar with the history of labyrinths and appreciated fully their symbolical significance. As an artist and lover of flowers, he contributed to the beauty of the Labyrinth as he did to everything in the community. It is said that he carved with his own hands the symbol of a wreath and a rose that was placed in the millennial arch of the brick church.

It may be said here that Frederick Rapp was indispensable to the successful direction of the Society's affairs as its business and financial agent. He was its main contact with the outside world in commerce, diplomacy, and statesmanship. In 1816, he was elected one of the four delegates from Gibson County to the Indiana Constitutional Convention. Gibson County then included the northern part of Posey County in which New Harmony is situated. Frederick was one of the forty-three delegates from Indiana's thirteen counties, who met at Corydon, under the old Elm Tree, from June 10 to June 29, 1816, and framed the first constitution of the State. In 1820 he was chosen by the State Legislature as one of the eight commissioners to select the site of Indianapolis as the seat of the new capital of the State.

His genius entered into every phase of community life, even to occupying the pulpit occasionally at church meetings in the absence of Father Rapp. He lived in the house of Father Rapp during their ten years on the Wabash and was at all times his capable and trusted lieutenant. Many of the most important activities of the community were conducted upon his own responsibility as the temporal head.

A large, handsome man of the most lovable qualities, he devoted himself unselfishly all his life to the welfare of the community and to the cultivation of friendship and harmony. He composed some of the hymns of the Society that were the most popular then and best known today. John S. Duss wrote of him:

> He was an artisan, an architect of ability, a connoisseur in matters of art, a musician; upon the whole, a man possessed of about as much ability and as many virtues, as can well be housed in one human temple —altogether a prince among men.

GERTRUDE RAPP

(1808-1889)

IT is fitting to make special mention here of a revered female member of the Harmony Society. Gertrude Rapp, granddaughter of Father George Rapp, by his only son John, was an outstanding Harmonist from early childhood and was better known throughout her life than any other woman of the Society.

She was born in old Harmonie, Pennsylvania, in 1808. Because of the death of her father when she was a small child, she made her home with her grandfather as long as he lived; and then continued to live in the Great House at Economy, Pennsylvania, as its mistress, until her own death there forty-two years later. She was seven years of age when the Society came to the Wabash and seventeen when they left.

Young William Owen became well acquainted with her during his five months stay with the Rappites in their last days on the Wabash. His diary from December 16, 1824 to April 20, 1825, shows that he visited the Rapp home on twenty-seven different days. He made frequent mention of Gertrude, describing her as:

> "a very natural and pretty girl of 15 or 16 . . . pretty, unaffected, good-humored and with great simplicity of character . . . a good specimen of Harmony training."

She often sang for him and played on the pianoforte.

The best characterization of her is to be found in the writings of John S. Duss, who knew her long and well. He wrote, in part:

> Little Gertrude was always in high favor not only with her grandfather, but with the entire Society. The leading men, such as Frederick Rapp, John L. Baker and R. L. Baker, when absent on business trips to Philadelphia, New York, and other points, always wrote letters to Gertrude. Manifestly the Society's queen, she was the recipient of more adulation on the part of its members than was accorded to any other person throughout its entire history. That, in spite of all this, she was at all times modest, unassuming, sweet tempered and perfectly natural, entitles her to the highest encomiums that can be paid to any person.
>
> Her education comprised the German, English and French languages; mathematics, painting, embroidery, and the manufacture of wax fruits and flowers. Her passion was music, and in this she received careful training, both vocal and instrumental. She had many friends without the Society with whom she carried on a considerable correspondence.

She was all her life possessed of personal beauty and loveliness of character, even in her old age attracting the attention of visitors. For many years, the dignified and gracious mistress of the "Great House" (house of Father Rapp and the succeeding trustee) it was my privilege for twenty-five years to know this admirable woman, and I wish to state she is the only person I ever knew who was a strong character, of whom all, both friend and foe, spoke but in terms of admiration.

No wonder that one historian remarks: "To have produced even one such character would be enough honor to any community."

During the conduct of the silk mill in Economy, as an important industry of the Harmony Society, Gertrude was its efficient superintendent. She was, indeed, an ideal Harmonist throughout a long and useful life.

Gertrude passed away in 1889 at the age of eighty-one.

THE CHURCHES

IT was natural that the Rappite churches should have been the most outstanding structures of the community. There were two of them, one of frame and the other of brick. The frame church, which was erected in 1816, was a two story building, seventy-five feet long, fifty feet wide and fifty feet high. It had a large belfry, which contained a clock eight feet in diameter. A system of bells, somewhat in the nature of chimes, was connected with the clock so as to toll the hours and quarters. The large bell that tolled the hours could be heard seven miles. The quarters were sounded by a smaller bell. The lofty steeple containing the clock and the bells was destroyed by lightning some years after the Rappites left and the entire building was taken down in 1836.

The beautiful brick church, built in the form of a Maltese Cross, with four wings or entrances, was erected in 1822. It was indeed a temple in the wilderness. The tradition already mentioned was well established that it was constructed according to a design which came to Father Rapp in a dream or vision three different times. Certainly it expressed the nobility of Rappite faith as well as something of the grandeur of the mysticism of Father Rapp and the architectural genius of Frederick Rapp. The main part of the building consisted of a large hall or auditorium, eighty feet square. There were four wings each closed by folding doors, which were about one hundred twenty feet from each other. The upper story was supported by twenty-eight doric columns made of immense walnut, cherry, and sassafras trees. The walnut pillars were larger than the others, being six feet in circumference and twenty-five feet high. The others were twenty-one feet high and a little over five feet in circumference. They surrounded the big central room in which all regular services were held and which was large enough to accommodate every member of the community at a single seating. The huge columns that encircled this room gave it a very solemn and impressive appearance. All services were usually attended by all members of the Society. Frequently there were all-day services on Sunday and usually on one or more nights each week.

The millennial arch was placed at the entrance to the north wing. This church was not removed entirely until 1874. It stood where the New Harmony schoolhouse now stands. William Hebert, an English traveller, wrote of it:

> "I can scarcely imagine myself to be in the woods of Indiana, on the borders of the Wabash, while facing the long resounding aisles and surveying the stately colonnades of this church."

It is fitting, indeed, that most of the bricks of which it was built still memorialize its sturdy builders in the strong wall that surrounds the cemetery.

The frame church was immediately east of it. It was characteristic of the thrift and practicality of the Rappites that parts of both of these churches were used at times for material purposes such as the storing of grain and other supplies. The fact that a pioneer community in the wilderness in that early day would maintain two such structures for religious activities, speaks volumes as to the emphasis the Rappites placed upon spiritual life.

The symbolism of the great brick temple—formed as a Maltese Cross— was most impressive. It may be noted in this connection that a pleasing tradition has long prevailed in New Harmony concerning another way in which the Harmony Society symbolized the cross in their so-called "Christian Doors." In nearly all of the buildings, and especially in the larger homes, there were doors in which some upper panels were drawn in such a way as to constitute a simple form of the cross. The tradition has grown that these were intended as "Christian Doors," in the belief that only Christian blessings could enter them. Whether or not the Rappites did make a special symbolical feature of those doors, it is certain that they were used very generally. There seems to be no mechanical reason why the cross should have been formed in that fashion.

Many of the original "Christian Doors" are to be found both in Economy and New Harmony today. Such a tradition is a becoming re-flection of the symbolism of the members of the Harmony Society attach-ing to the cross.

THE BRICK CHURCH

THE MILLENNIUM

BELIEF in the early coming of the millennium was a cornerstone in the religious foundation of the "House of Harmony." Father Rapp sincerely believed that to him would be vouchsafed the privilege of presenting his people to Christ, at the second coming. He lived and taught this belief consistently, and it seems to have been adopted by all his followers, although no formal written statement of it appears in the explanation of their creed.

Dr. Aaron Williams, in his brief history written in 1866, says that even before leaving Germany the members who later formed the Harmony Society "had generally adopted the millennarian theory of the personal and pre-millennial advent of Christ, which they regarded as near at hand." They bore themselves as if they expected to be called at any time. This must have had great effect upon their spiritual thought, even though it did not apparently affect their concern as to material needs; that is, it certainly did not make them less provident. Following the inherent principles of their sturdy character they looked after all material wants, both for the present and future. Their sturdy buildings were erected in the only manner in which they knew how to build. They were so substantially constructed that after more than a century they still stand firm and unyielding to the ravages of time, even though their builders did not expect to occupy them long.

In their practical application of their millennial doctrine, they looked upon it as the ushering in of the golden age upon earth which would constitute the best preparation for the ascension that they thought was approaching. Their creed recites:

> The philanthropist however must not despair, for every thing what-
> ever, which the men of God have foretold, is nevertheless fully
> approaching; everything is pressing forward to the near advanced
> better time; he has only vigorously to surmount the obstacles, which
> come in his way. The day of the Lord is drawing near, and will
> dominate over all that is high, and humiliate all which is lofty. Jesus
> Christ the universal supreme regent will unite all contraries together,
> for every thing always takes its direction towards Him. Wise and
> enlightened men even know already, how to unite and bring in order
> the same contraries; because the knowledge of nature and religion
> appears open and clear to their eyes, and they perceive plainly the
> golden age, in its near approach.

In other words, they held the sane and logical view that only the attainment of material harmony could herald the coming of the millennium.

> For as soon as true and sincere fraternities of harmonious minds are formed and come to appearance, and who know how to unite the spiritual matters with the physical, in an indissoluble preservation, for the promotion both of an inward and outward happiness, there immediately the mountains do proclaim peace, and the hills righteousness, and darkness flies before the light of day, because what men heretofore could not comprehend on account of the obscurity, is now manifest and clear, that this is the happiest enjoyment of life of every other. And the light is of course put upon the candlestick, and the town is built upon a mountain, where it may visibly be seen by all whose eyes are not blinded by a cloud.

They considered that the harmonious union which they were effecting in all their temporal and spiritual interests constituted the beginning of the millennium.

> The time is now at hand, where improved humanity is to transport all its various sensations, exertions, thoughts and sentiments, into the treasury of the common fund. Are not circumstances everywhere operating for its accomplishment? Is there not a good beginning made to it?

William Owen, in his diary, December 18, 1824, gives an account of the church service, which was conducted by Frederick Rapp in the absence of Father Rapp. In a discourse of an hour's length, as recorded by William Owen—

> He spoke from Isaiah regarding the millennium, which he considered to have commenced 30 odd years ago; that they were the commencement and that it consisted in men living together as brothers, each for all, all for each.

The Harmonists were constantly exhorted to aspire to the highest reach of perfection in their daily life in the fixed belief that by such living the golden age would be speedily ushered in.

> To what pinnacle of perfection dost thou aspire, thou better race of man! It is our exalted period alone, that can take such a high flight, and disseminate the blessings of the golden age. What a magnificent creation! And who would yet deny the possibility of its existence?

Although no authorized mention of any exact time for the ascension is to be found in the records of the Harmony Society, it is certain that Father Rapp believed that the ascension would come during his lifetime. He was 67 years of age when they left their home on the Wabash for their new home at Economy, Pennsylvania. The fact that they required

THE BUILDERS OF THE LABYRINTH

Robert Owen to give bond providing for the care of the cemetery *for only twenty years* is record evidence that they expected the millennium within that time. Sometime after their arrival in Economy, $510,000.00 of gold and silver and several hundred thousand pounds of baked flour were stored away to provide food and expense of transportation for the final pilgrimage, which Father Rapp believed would have to be made to the Holy Land, from which the ascension would occur. Surely this is material proof of the sincerity of his belief. When his end finally came in 1847, the gold and the flour were still intact. The board of elders who succeeded Father Rapp found sometime later that the flour was getting musty, and they had it converted into good whiskey, which they sold at the highest market price. During the Civil War the gold was converted into greenbacks at a premium.

Father Rapp's last reported words expressed his abiding faith in the millennium. After a short sermon from his bed, propped up by pillows, so that he could speak in a hoarse whisper to those outside the window, he said: "If I did not know that the dear Lord meant that I should present you all to him, I should think my last moment had come."

As explained elsewhere in this brochure, the Rappites symbolized their faith in the approaching millennium in a most fragrant manner, through the cultivation of beautiful flowers. There can be no doubt that the building and maintenance of the Labyrinth, which contained many flowering shrubs and trees, was a material part of this symbolism. It was also signalized beautifully in the millennial arch, which was artistically drawn by Frederick Rapp, with the adornment of a wreath and a rose, and with the citation, Micha 4:v8. Literally interpreted from the Lutheran Bible, this verse reads: "Unto thee shall come a golden rose, the first dominion." This millennial arch has been preserved with its supporting portals and doors and now stands at the west entrance of the New Harmony school building, near the spot where it was placed in the great brick temple.

The poetic call of the Rappite night watchman, as he made his rounds, "droning the hours," was vocal with millennial spirit:

> Again a day is passed and a step made nearer the end. Our time runs away and the joys of heaven are our reward.

THE FOOTPRINT ROCK

IN relation to the Labyrinth, it is appropriate to consider the Footprint Rock, which has come to be looked upon as a distinctive phenomenon of the Rappite regime in Harmonie. It has, indeed, received more emphasis from writers of history, folklore, and fiction who have touched upon New Harmony, than its historic importance justifies. However, this is a significant fact in itself. It must be that this importance has developed naturally because of the association of the Footprint Rock with the well established mysticism of Father Rapp. The tradition prevails, and will no doubt be cherished always, that the prints were made in the solid rock by the feet of the Angel Gabriel, who came to deliver a message to Father Rapp. There is, however, no historical evidence that Father Rapp ever made such a claim.

The rock was in the main yard of his residence some years before the Rappites left Harmonie. It had already attracted a good deal of attention from visitors and from some scientific students. Schoolcraft made extensive research and comment concerning it in 1821, from which, he argued the probability that the prints "were caused by the pressure of an individual that belonged to an unknown race of men." He regarded it as a world wonder.

In the diary of William Owen we find this note on December 19, 1824:

> In a back yard we saw a stone with the mark of two feet upon it, with a ring in front, supposed to have been made by an Indian before the stone was hardened: Mr. Rapp found it upon the Mississippi and sent some men to hew it from the rock.

Dr. David Dale Owen, geologist, is authority for the scientific conclusion that the Footprint Rock is limestone of the palaeozoic age and that the foot prints were the work of human hands.

Such legends as that of the Angel Gabriel leaving his foot prints imbedded in solid stone as a reminder of his visit to Father Rapp are evidence of the manner in which mystic sentiments are cherished among all peoples. There is a mystic interest in the legend of the Footprint Rock in New Harmony which may always be felt in connection with the life of the simple patriarch, Father George Rapp.

It may be looked upon as a symbol having traditional relationship with the mystic associations that surround the Rappite Labyrinth and other tokens of the devoted founders of that community on the Wabash.

CELIBACY

THE practice of celibacy in the Harmony Society has probably received more public attention than any other feature; in fact, it was noticed in a facetious way by Lord Byron in Canto XV of his *Don Juan*. Commenting upon Father Rapp's "embargo" of marriage as a fact of world-wide interest, the poet says, in part:

> Why call'd he "Harmony" a state sans wedlock?
> Now here I have got the preacher at a deadlock.
>
> Because he either meant to sneer at harmony
> Or marriage, by divorcing them thus oddly.

It may be assumed that this strange custom had intimate correlation with the Rappite belief in the early coming of the millennium. That impression was communicated to William Owen. In his diary, he makes the following notation, March 30, 1825, of a talk with Dr. Muller, the school master:

> He told me today that marriage is not forbidden amongst them, but as they expect Christ to reappear soon, they wish to be pre-pared, to meet him in a fit state, which could not be if they were taken up by sensual pleasures.

Certainly there is a logical if not a natural sequence between the millennial theory and celibacy. If the world was to end soon, why bring any more people into the world? Why propagate the species? It may be believed that the faithful Harmonists regarded such asceticism as direct preparation for the second advent of the Messiah—the resurrection, in which "they neither marry nor are given in marriage."

There is some uncertainty as to just how, when, and why the practice started. It is to be remembered that when the foundations of the Society were laid through the preaching of Father Rapp in Wurttemberg those who became members were then living in the normal state of wedlock. It seems that the practice developed gradually and was adopted generally in 1807, after which there were to be no further marriages, and those who were already married were to live as brothers and sisters in Christ.

John S. Duss, who lived among the elder members in their last days at Economy, is authority for the statement that marriage was never prohibited absolutely and that the celibate rule was probably subject to rare relaxation within the Society; but he asserts the positive conclusion that "the custom became prevalent and the birth rate almost nil."

Dr. Aaron Williams made the following explanation of celibacy:

> The practice of celibacy was also only a more full and consistent carrying out of the fundamental principles of entire equality in all things, which implied an abstinence on the part of individuals from every indulgence in which all alike might not participate.

Certainly there was ample Scriptural support for this custom such, for example, as the precept of the Apostle Paul:

> This I say, brethren, the time is short: it remaineth that both they that have wives be as though they had none.

Regardless of any other consideration of fact or theory, it is well established, so far as the outside world knew, that this strange contravention of one of the most compelling laws of human nature was observed during their ten years' stay on the Wabash with a consistency that was, indeed, creditable to the sincerity of those Harmonists.

All this is subject to some interesting reflections. What was the effect upon the community and upon the members individually? The effect upon the women is of especial importance for it gave them peculiar independence. Relieved of the burden of childbirth and child rearing, they became productive on equal terms with the men. They worked with the men; they worked like the men, and—it was said—became as strong as the men. Under such circumstances they did with apparent ease and satisfaction many types of work that were then (and are even yet) considered masculine. The women sheared the sheep. They did nearly all of the work in the factories, the cotton and woolen mills. They worked in the fields, especially at harvest time, side by side with the men, rhythmically swinging their shining sickles, timed by the music of the band.

The dormitory life of a large portion of the men and the functioning of community ovens relieved the women of much of the heavy house work. It may be believed that they were able to devote unusual attention to the cultivation of flowers and to the enjoyment of music. The psychological bearing of all this offers a field for both psychic and mystic speculation.

It is possible that these devoted Harmonists realized the benefits of sublimation to a very high degree. They may have transferred the psychical energy of sex impulse into loftier creative expression. Their natural emotional cravings may have found happy expression not only in their material thrift but in their spiritual enjoyments and in their pleasing diversions of floral and musical culture.

The four large brick dormitories that the Rappites built for the housing of single men were material symbols of their practice of celibacy. Of these unique buildings, which were numbered 1, 2, 3, and 4, the last three are still standing as significant Memorial units.

THE KINGDOM OF FLOWERS

NOTHING could be more happily significant in connection with the lofty faith of the Harmonists in the coming of the millennium than their flower culture. This, together with their enlivening and impressive music, is regarded as their only diversion. It was, indeed, an appropriate diversion. Flowers are emblems of the resurrection, symbols of a brighter and better land. The Rappites grew them everywhere in the community—in all the gardens and around the dwellings and in addition kept them in their factories and work shops, where potted plants hung upon the walls and vases of flowers were placed upon the tables. Indeed, it might be considered that they instituted a veritable kingdom of flowers—fragrant heraldry of their kingdom of Heaven upon earth.

It seems that the rose in all its lovely varieties was probably the favorite flower, as suggested in the symbol of the millennial arch. However, they cultivated every kind of flower that they found suited to the soil and climate. William Cobbett, who was a noted horticulturist and maintained fine gardens on Long Island, visited the Rappites in Harmonie for the purpose of observing their floral culture. In his journal he said:

> "I observe that these people are very fond of flowers, by the bye; the cultivation of them, and music, are their chief amusements. . . . Perhaps the pains they take with them is the cause of their flowers being finer than any I have hitherto seen in America; but most probably the climate is here more favorable. The houses are good and clean, and have, each one, a nice garden well stocked with flowers."

The explanation of their creed contains many references to flowers and other growing plants. It refers to the harmonious order of their BROTHERLY UNION as "a breath of heavenly life, visibly appearing in blossoms and fruits." It continues with this exhortation:

> Let us rejoice that it has fallen to our lot, to live in the present important era, when the plants of God in the Creation, appear in all their harmony, symmetry, order and unity, and when every thing in Nature, with incessant activity and renewed life, is pressing forward to a complete resemblance of the great Archetype.

The following allegory is significant:

> The seed which has originally been planted in the heart of man, has come up, sprouted and grown to a considerable plant, appearing

in a true godlike human form, whose beauty surpasses every terrestrial idea.

This is the real, true abode and great nursery, where soul and body find their desired object. The body remains here, the spirit continues to live with its deceased brethren, and the works begun here are continued as the Psalmist observes: "You are planted in the house of God, as a green olive tree growing and thriving forever."

As previously noted, Father Rapp maintained a large greenhouse and nursery in his own yard, both because of his love of floral culture and for the assistance that he could give in this manner to the dissemination of such culture throughout the community.

The Labyrinth may be regarded as a fine extension of their fragrant diversion. It was described by the Duke of Saxe-Weimar as a garden "exclusively devoted to flowers." On his visit to Economy less than two years after the Harmonists had settled there, the Duke recorded enthusiastically: "Fresh flowers greeted us everywhere, even on the work benches."

In death as in life, the Harmonists maintained association with flowers and growing plant life—flowers upon the caskets and the graves grassed over with no semblance of the tomb.

THE HARMONIOUS-SPIRIT

(Harmonische-Geist)

AS already noted, the religion of the Harmony Society is not easily grasped. It was not defined by creed or classified by formal doctrines. The Harmonists did not subscribe individually to any sectarian tenets. Their creed was the Bible. It is probable that all of them were in full agreement with the condensed maxim of Father Rapp, "Love to God above all and to thy neighbor as thyself." Within this broad conception there were no doubt various individual views as to special features of religious belief.

However, all Harmonists united in cherishing what they called the Harmonious-Spirit (Harmonische-Geist.) This was well stated in a letter by John S. Duss, November 21, 1938:

> Here is something that no outsider ever knew or could understand. This Society of different individuals and faiths, had one indefinable thing in common which can only be understood by one whose daily life was among these people, and that is a SPIRIT—the "Harmonious-Spirit" (Harmonische-Geist). This term had a meaning and influence all its own, and was felt more strongly than the term "Holy Spirit" or "Holy Ghost." You can perhaps understand this when you come to think of it as being a part of the practical daily life. The members in referring to other members would say such and such an one had more or less of "The Harmonious-Spirit."
>
> And here is another surprise. People formerly connected with the Harmony Society, such as the hired help or in business, several years ago, with my assistance, formed what we call The Economy Old Timers. Said organization meets every year on June 6, the day that the advance guard of The Harmony Society arrived from the Wabash in 1824. At these meetings this same "Harmonious-Spirit" is powerfully manifest and there is much wonderment about a peculiar something that no one has ever found at the meeting of family groups or clans. The matter to me is as plain as the ABC's. The SPIRIT that prevails is that same "Harmonische-Geist" of the years gone by.

It was natural that such a spirit flowered into a state of perfect friendship among the members of the Harmony Society. It was given many gracious expressions in the Thoughts of Father Rapp.

> The golden treasure of this world, to those who know how to preserve it, is Friendship.

THE BUILDERS OF THE LABYRINTH

Again we read:

> How sacred and dear is friendship, it is a glowing fire of recreative undefiled brotherly flame! Cheerful and concordant, she springs up to animate union of a firm, faithful, indivisible philanthropy and brotherly love.

We also find a religious extension of this sentiment as follows:

> Such a friendship is heavenly and rises into Deity. As all hearts are open towards each other, the spirit flows together, in a pure and perfect unity which is in God.

The following is a statement of its practical workings:

> God requires no more of any human being than one man of honour and reputation requires of another.

Perhaps the most concrete demonstration of the prevalence of this Harmonious-Spirit is found in the universal practice of the Harmonists, of scrupulously avoiding any kind of personal controversy as far as possible. It was a ruling principle among them to try to avoid having the last word. They looked upon those who withdrew from heated arguments first as being the best exponents of the Harmonious-Spirit. This custom was climaxed fittingly in the slogan "Let not the sun go down upon your wrath."

We must see in all this a genuine inauguration within the Society of what they conceived to be a bright kingdom of peace on earth, good will to men. It created a vital philosophy that was reflected, of course, in all phases of their conduct, as the *Thoughts* express it:

> That divine philosophy which harmoniously combines the spiritual and temporal concerns of life, requires no arbitrary laws. Those good men who are influenced by its doctrines always do, without compulsion, that which they know is right, merely from their love of virtue.

The Harmonious-Spirit was a fine extension of the golden rule which received due recognition from all those outside the Society who had intimate dealings with its members. Robert Owen paid this tribute to the Rappites as he found them in Harmonie:

> It is due to the Society who formed this settlement to state that I have not yet met with more kind-hearted, temperate, and industrious citizens, nor found men more sincere, upright, and honest in all dealings, than the Harmonists.

[73]

HARMONIST FESTIVALS

THE Harmony Society observed three great annual festivals or feast days. These were the Organization Celebration in February, usually the 15th; Harvest Home Festival early in August; and the Love Feast in October. These days were Harmonist days strictly. They were annual holidays. The exercises consisted principally of feasting and music along with some talking. They continued throughout the entire day and evening and were attended by every member of the Society.

William Owen gives an account in his diary of the Organization Day Celebration held in old Harmonie on the Wabash, February 17, 1825. The regular day was February 15, the anniversary of the formal founding of the Harmony Society, February 15, 1805. This particular feast was the 20th anniversary. Owen's report of it is as follows:

> This day the Harmonians celebrated the 20th anniversary of their union into a society. They began with music between five and six o'clock and at 9 they went to church; at 12 they dined and remained together with a short interval until near five o'clock; and at 6 they supped and remained together till after 9 o'clock.
>
> What they were engaged in we did not learn as they kept it to themselves, but they seemed to think they had passed the day agreeably, and from many expressions which they made use of, I should conclude that the meeting, from some cause or other, had tended to strengthen the bond of Union subsisting among them. Part of the day was probably employed in getting a knowledge of the state of their affairs. They have now been united 20 years. They transacted no business at the store but many persons arrived on business and were disappointed as they had not given any notice of the intended holiday before. This the Americans thought they should have done. But they seemed to wish to throw a veil of secrecy over all their proceedings. Before breaking up at 5 o'clock, they marched out of the church in closed ranks preceded by their music, all singing. They halted before Mr. Rapp's house and sang a piece of music and then dispersed.

The Harvest Home Festival in August was a jubilant celebration of the harvest time. It was a form of rejoicing over the rich yield of the good earth in bountiful crops—an expression of gratitude to providence for rewarding their industry. On this occasion, particularly, and perhaps equally so on both of the others, there was a veritable cornucopia of good things to eat and drink—the richest of foods and the finest of wines. As noted in the diary of William Owen, they began early in the morning between 5 and 6 o'clock and continued throughout the day and evening until after 9.

The feasting on each of these days was attended with a great deal of music, both vocal and instrumental. The music hall, which they built at Economy and which is well preserved today, was used almost entirely for feasting and music. The lower floor was given over to the band but the upper floor was used especially for these annual feasts. Immediately adjoining the music hall is the old kitchen still preserved with its huge ovens and twelve large kettles. The principal diet for these feasts was a rare stew which consisted mainly of veal and rice deliciously seasoned. Preparations were begun several days in advance of the feasts and they were looked forward to with much zest by all Harmonists. The October festival, known as the Love Feast, was a symbolical observance of the Lord's Supper.

These three days were well distributed throughout the year so that they constituted a delightful round of wholesome enjoyment. We may well believe that such festive occasions contributed vastly to the Harmonious-Spirit (Harmonische-Geist).

MUSIC

IT may be said that music was the chief recreation of the Harmonists. However, it meant much more to them than recreation. They loved music and attended to its cultivation. Every member of the community had musical training and nearly all of them could play some musical instrument. Of course, all could sing. They sang at their work as well as at all kinds of gatherings. They sometimes improvised as they sang. Many of their songs were of a solemn and impressive character, generally with a deeply religious strain. However, they also enjoyed some lighter songs and some livelier instrumental numbers. The songs were usually devoted to a spirit of friendship.

Visitors were regaled with music both vocal and instrumental on all occasions. William Owen records that on their first day in Harmonie, Indiana, December 17, 1824, he and his father dined with Frederick Rapp at the home of George Rapp, who had then gone to Economy, and that Father Rapp's granddaughter—

> Gertrude, a very pretty, innocent young girl of 15 or 16, after dinner played some airs on the pianoforte and sang a few German songs, along with 3 other girls, also very good looking, whom Mr. Rapp sent for.

In the afternoon, they visited the cotton mill, which was driven by oxen walking on an incline plane. The diary records:

> The mill stopped to let them rest and while we waited till the shower was over, the women in the room formed a circle and sang several songs to us of their own accord. The words are usually about friendship and harmony and the music is their own. Those who work together learn to sing with each other, thus forming a number of small singing parties.

Perhaps no better contemporaneous reflection of Rappite music could be found than in this diary of William Owen. Even at the risk of tediousness, some of the running comments of this observant young Scotchman made from day to day, from December 16, 1824 to April 20, 1825, are worth noting. Only brief excerpts can be quoted:

—Sunday, December 19, 1824—

> We dined at 11 and at ½ p. 12 we were summoned to church by the band playing different airs. When we were all seated different parties of men and women sang hymns etc. for an hour; the band assisting occasionally.

THE BUILDERS OF THE LABYRINTH

At 5 o'clock evening it was still light. We returned to tea with Mr. Rapp, or rather to an elegant supper, composed of all sorts of meats, cakes, etc. Afterwards, in an adjoining room, music commenced and we had a concert of vocal and instrumental music till 9 o'clock. There were 21 singers and a piano forte, 2 violins and 2 flutes and a bass.

—Sunday, January 16, 1825—

No sermon in the church, owing to Mr. Rapp's absence. The principal observable occupation of the Harmonians was music, which they carried on in small parties in different parts of the village.

—Friday, January 21—

After dinner we called on Mrs. Rapp and Miss Gertrude, who sang Auld Lang Syne to us. Dr. Muller came in and assisted.

—Thursday, February 17—

This day the Harmonians celebrated the 20th anniversary of their union into a society. They began with music between five and six o'clock and at 9 they went to church; at 12 they dined and remained together with a short interval until near five o'clock.

Before breaking up at 5 o'clock, they marched out of the church in closed ranks preceded by their music, all singing. They halted before Mr. Rapp's house and sang a piece of music and then dispersed.

—Sunday, February 20—

In the evening we were invited by Mr. Rapp to take tea with him, We met there Mrs. and Miss Gertrude Rapp, Mrs. John Rapp (Gertrude's mother), Caroline Beiser, the housemaid, and George, the hostler.

After tea, Dr. Muller came in, also several performers on different instruments and a number of female singers; whereupon a concert commenced which lasted until half past nine.

—Sunday, February 27—

After dinner the Harmonians assembled to the call of the bugle and at Mr. Rapp's invitation we joined them. We walked, preceded by music and occasionally singing, to the vineyards, into one of which we entered. In the center of one is an open space, from which leads an alley overhung by vines. Here we remained for some time listening to the Harmonians band.

Afterwards we returned with music as we had come.

—Friday, March 18—

Between twelve and one o'clock, the steamboat (William Penn) set sail with fifty or sixty Harmonians having fired a salute in answer to the musical band, which being collected on the shore, played several pieces.

—Sunday, March 20—

At one o'clock we attended a musical meeting in the church and afterwards walked through the house and garden of Mr. Rapp. In the evening, we supped there with Mr. & Mrs. and Miss Gertrude Rapp. Afterwards, a good deal of music. A very fine day.

THE LABYRINTH

The Duke of Saxe-Weimar followed his visit to New Harmony under the Owenite regime in April, 1826 with a visit to Economy, where the Rappites had been in their new settlement for a little less than two years. In his journal, he made several comments upon the musical entertainment they gave him. For example, as he neared the settlement, "three hornists played a melody of welcome." After supper at Rapp's home, "he (Rapp) called together the musicians of the Society to entertain us with music. Also, Miss Gertrude (Rapp's granddaughter) played the piano and three girls sang."

On the next day, Rapp took him to the factory to hear "the girls, some sixty or seventy, sing songs, first of a religious, then of a gay character." He characterized the songs as "extraordinarily good and remarkably well arranged." Of his last day there, he wrote: "Again we ate a hearty dinner, the orchestra played really excellently, and it was with quite peculiar emotions that we departed, at three o'clock, from the friendly and industrious town of Economy."

It is fortunate indeed that John S. Duss, who is mentioned frequently in these pages, is still living (1941) and very alert mentally in his eighty-second year. His extensive memoirs, which will be published soon, will contain invaluable morsels of history on every feature of the Harmony Society and especially upon the subject of music.

Being possessed of rare musical talent, Mr. Duss gave special attention to the music of the Harmony Society. He organized and conducted the famous Economy Band in 1902 which played throughout the season in New York. The orchestra that he directed at Madison Square Garden was the outstanding musical attraction of the metropolis during the summers of 1903 and 1904. As one of America's noted musical conductors and composers, Mr. Duss has been able to demonstrate to the world the rare musical genius of the Harmony Society. He possesses many of the original instruments, books, manuscripts, and other musical data of the Society.

Notwithstanding his advanced age, he still wields a bewitching baton. This was delightfully demonstrated on the Memorial occasion of the Octo-Millennial Celebration in New Harmony, June 23, 1939, which was reported in the *New Harmony Times*, June 30, in part, as follows:

> The celebration of the One Hundred Twenty-fifth Birthday of New Harmony last Friday, June 23, was a great and well deserved triumph for Mr. John S. Duss, and a fine treat to the people of New Harmony. This was very properly Mr. Duss' own occasion. We were very glad indeed to have it so. He arranged and directed all the important features of the program and was, himself, the principal feature in our eyes. There is no other person living who could have

done what he did all in his own person. Through his mastery of music together with his intimate knowledge of the great historic theme of the day, he exemplified the true and living spirit of that band of pioneers, the Harmony Society, better known to us as Rappites, who founded that first famous settlement here on the Wabash in June, 1814.

The evening meeting was indeed a climax of musical interpretation. Mr. Duss had prepared and arranged a group of great numbers mostly of his own composition or adaptation. They expressed better than any historic chronicle could possibly express, the spirit and meaning of old Harmonie as it existed here a century and a quarter ago. He not only directed the playing and singing of these numbers but also gave dramatic recitals in connection with several of them.

There were six principal numbers rendered in the following order: Harmonie Thou Flower Fair, Ye Gentle Harmonites, New Harmony All Hail, The Cross and Crown, O Come All Ye Faithful, and Children of Friendship and Love.

Mr. Duss orated with stirring effect the "Cross and Crown" which he had composed in 1896 for the Hugh de Payne's Commandery K. of P., Milrose, Mass. Both the words and the music of the last number, "Children of Friendship and Love," had been composed by Frederick Rapp, to whom Mr. Duss paid a lofty tribute for his mysticism and his genius.

Mr. Duss made a very impressive appearance in his capacity as director of both the vocal and instrumental music. Proudly decorated with the handsome medal of gold and diamonds presented him 36 years ago by the Metropolitan Orchestra of Madison Square Garden, he wielded a masterly baton in a manner that brought back memories of the great days of Sousa, Damrosch and Duss of more than a generation ago.

A fitting climax of the evening came in the presentation of a silver loving cup to Mr. Duss by his numberless friends of New Harmony.

The following comments concerning the music of the Harmony Society are adapted from the yet unpublished memoirs of Mr. Duss and from his recent correspondence. The limitations of space permit only brief extracts; but sufficient, it is hoped, to exhibit the real inherent genius that the Harmony Society had for music and the vital part it played in the community.

Mr. Duss came into early appreciation of it. He says:

My introducton to the Harmony Society music at its best was when in August, 1862, at the age of 2½ years, my mother took me to the Ernte-Fest (Harvest Home). That affair to me was heaven on earth and the music by the orchestra heaven itself.

He lived in the homes of some of the leading musicians, in which his mother was housekeeper, and grew up under their inspiration and instruction in music. He was a very apt pupil, playing several different instruments—accordion, cornet, violin, snare drum, clarinet, harmonium (parlor organ), etc. At the age of six, he was the "boy wonder" at playing the accordion—a proficiency developed without any teacher whatsoever. People came from far and near to hear him.

The special festivals of the Society, partly religious in character, were celebrated with feasting and music. Of these, Mr. Duss makes the following comment:

> Worthy of especial notice are the matinal concerts of Christmas, Anniversary (Feb. 15th), Easter and Pentecost.
>
> On these festal days, before the dawn, the Band climbed the stairs to the church-tower balcony, there to bring to the sleeping community the great delight of awakening to strains of melody from heaven.
>
> I can testify to that, for of all the music that I ever heard, the music that floated from the church-tower balcony at Economy, is outstanding in sweetness and delight.
>
> On the aforementioned days, as well as on Thanksgiving Day, there were held three meetings in Church—morning, afternoon and evening. The afternoon and evening services consisted almost entirely of music, and most of it by the band. True, the mixed choir and at times a chorus of men's voices were heard, but the chief performance was that of the instrumentalists.
>
> At the afternoon and evening sessions of the Society's Feasts (Feb. 15th, Harvest Home, and Love-Feast) it was about the same. The Tower-balcony music was dispensed two numbers from each corner, so that every section got its full share. The music was lively in character, as was that given on other occasions. There were marches, waltzes, polkas, minuets, all kinds of dance music, and selections containing song melodies adapted to words of a low order.
>
> One of the most picturesque affairs at Economy, was the annual pilgrimage to the Society's grave yard. This took place, whenever it was feasible, when the appletrees were in full bloom. One should have this arrival of the gaily bedizened Harmonist men (in frock coats of blue silk and Harmonist women in red, white and blue kerchief, blue silk shirt and Normandy bonnet of variegated silks) in techni-color. One can form somewhat of an idea of the beauty of the scene at the cemetery located under the appletrees of the orchard.
>
> The parade formed in the center of the village. Starting at the church, led by the hand, the procession to the strains of a dirge, wended its way to the cemetery. Here one of the trustees delivered a short address. After some verses from an appropriate hymn (by band and audience) the march continued to an Indian burial mound located a short distance ahead. Here followed more remarks and more music, after which came the march homeward. But this home-ward procession was not to funeral tempo, but to liveliest of quick steps.
>
> On the Fourth of July the band assembled on the upper veranda of the Economy Hotel and held forth with patriotic and other selec-tions, chiefly for the benefit of visitors from Pittsburgh and other points.
>
> Weather permitting, at midnight of Dec. 31, the band on each square hailed the New Year. On this day the afternoon and evening services were of the same concert character as those of Christmas.

THE BUILDERS OF THE LABYRINTH

The kind and variety of music enjoyed by the Harmonists is shown in their original music books, some of them in manuscript, which Mr. Duss has in his possession. Of the Flute Book of the Harmony Society Orchestra, he writes:

> This Flute Book indicates that the orchestra was well prepared for all occasions or emergencies. There are 312 numbers and 14 specials —solos, duets, quartettes, etc.
>
> These selections include patriotic American numbers together with marches and waltzes galore from many different countries. Some of them are dedicated to individuals of great prominence, such as Washington, Jackson, Monroe, Lafayette, Napoleon, the Emperor of Russia, Duke of York, Maria Louisa, etc.
>
> Dance music is prevalent in variety. Among it beautiful Minuets by Mozart and Beethoven and Haydn. Of many waltzes, some are by Mozart. Several Quadrilles and a Polonaise by Ch. von Bonnhorst (a Pittsburgh composer and friend of the Society), and Hornpipes, as the Irish Washerwoman. The last number—312—is entitled "A Lively Dance." Most of the numbers do not have the composer's name; it is therefore impossible to determine how many of them were composed by members of the Society.
>
> It is not to be wondered at why the composers' names are not in evidence. When one recalls that during the first twenty-five years of the Society's existence the members cut down three virgin forests, built three towns and cleared thousands of acres for cultivation, etc., etc., it can be readily understood why these people eschewed every least task that was not absolutely necessary. Hence when it came to writing or copying music (where even the lines of the staff had to be drawn by hand) the name of the composer became of little amount— particularly when they all knew his name. The hymns for church service (some of them) had been set to music in the early days by Dr. J. Ch. Muller (the schoolmaster). Some of the melodies were not known by him so he got them from members who could "hum the tunes." This, as well as the "humming" of original compositions, brought results which were at times astonishing.

He makes further reference to original compositions of the Harmonists in the realm of music and poetry as follows:

> Reverting to the arduous toil of clearing land and building houses, these hardy pioneers nevertheless indulged in the extravagance of writing essays and poetry, exalting and extolling the importance, the wonders and the glory of HARMONIE (i. e. the Harmony Society). Inasmuch as poets and musicians were looked upon as superior beings, (Geo. Rapp was a born poet; Fredr. Rapp both poet and musician), many of the lay members undertook to write poetry—some, more intrepid, even composed the music to their poetic effusions. The results were, as one might expect: good, bad and indifferent.

Mr. Duss makes special mention of a music book, published at Harmonie on the Wabash, entitled *A Collection of Various Piano-*

THE LABYRINTH

Pieces, Progressively Arranged For Gertrude Rapp.   Harmonie, Ind.,
July, 1823. He says:

> The entire volume is in manuscript—the handiwork of a painstaking
> individual.   It also shows the use of the music-pen (a device with
> 5 points for making the 5 lines of the staff at a single ruling).
>
> Beginning with very simple exercises, the 126 numbers—mostly
> popular music of the period—gradually increase in difficulty.
>
> Inasmuch as the Harmonists did not cultivate the terpsichorean art,
> the waltzes, polkas, minuets, quadrilles and hornpipes reach an astound-
> ing number; not only in this book for the piano forte but in the
> orchestra repertoire.   And they were used continuously in concerts
> indoors as well as out of doors.
>
> I am reminded here of a smaller volume of the year 1822—
> *Choral-Buch* For Gertrude Rapp, Harmonie, Ind., A. D. 1822.
> This book, all of it in manuscript of course, contains 54 of the best-
> known, standard German hymns and chorals and is arranged similarly
> to the *Collection*, mentioned above—beginning with simple easy
> arrangement and gradual ascendancy into the more difficult.

He takes pains to explain the wide range of variety of Harmonist
music:

> Although the Harmonists adapted many Old World melodies to
> their hymns, they practically excluded the magnificent CHORALS such
> as Luther's *A Mighty Fortress Is Our God.*   They had no patience
> with the slow, solemn tread of the sort of music which to them was
> representative of what they regarded as head hanging or downcast
> Christianity, in other words, HYPOCRISY.   Hence they went to the
> other extreme—adopting folksongs and street songs and, as to the
> ordinary dignified hymns, they added grace notes and turns and fur-
> belows, and speeded up the tempo until both dignity and HYPOCRISY
> were non est.
>
> True, there are a number of Minuets by Mozart, Beethoven, Pleyel;
> waltzes by Mozart, also other numbers by Haydn, etc.   But most
> of the music is of the ordinary type.   The great number of pieces
> of dance music therefore can only be credited to the leaning away
> from the stately, the dignified, the majestic, toward the lively and
> whatsoever was in lighter vein—the same tendency mentioned hereto-
> fore in connection with the music used in their religious service.

The following naive comment of Mr. Duss is illuminating as to
the Harmonian use of "song melodies adapted to words of a low order."

> I recall an incident in the 1870's, when one of the supercilious
> hired hands took it upon himself to remonstrate with Henrici about
> permitting the band to play this music "of the street and bawdy
> house."   Henrici, with a twinkle in his eye replied, "You evidently
> know things that are not interesting to me.   As for music itself, there
> is nothing low or impure therein, and in any case we are not going
> to let the Devil exercise preemptory rights when it comes to a question
> of ownership in the realm of music."   "Amen," said one and all to
> the Henrici summing up.

THE BUILDERS OF THE LABYRINTH

It should be said as to Jacob Henrici, who is mentioned in the above quotation and has been referred to previously, that he was for many years the foremost musician of the Harmony Society. Thoroughly trained in harmony in the old country, he joined the Society in Economy, as a young man, just when the colony was being established there in 1825 and soon became a leader, especially in music. He taught singing classes, performed creditably on the piano, occupied the chair of first violin in the orchestra and indulged somewhat in composition. As mentioned early in the brochure he became one of the two trustees of the Society upon the death of Father Rapp in 1847, and after the death of his fellow trustee, R. L. Baker, in 1868, became senior trustee and was practically the supreme head of the community from that time until his death in 1892. He came to New Harmony with the junior trustee, Jonathan Lenz, in 1874 and made arrangements for the transfer of the church ground to Harmony school township and for the building of the brick wall around the old cemetery.

Mr. Duss stresses the tendency of the songsters of Harmonie to extol the glory of Harmonie, itself, in their original oratorios and cantatas. He says:

> These oratorios and cantatas are powerfully reminiscent of the Psalms. But whereas the psalmodist of Holy Writ concerns himself with praise and eulogy of the MOST HIGH (God), the Harmonist lyricist outdoes himself in extolling the virtues, beauty, and advantages of Harmonie.
>
> Such exaltation and encomium, indeed, at times must strike the "uninitiated" as ad nauseum—in any case the incense-bearing censer wafts the Harmonie unto High Heaven.

He refers to specific examples, as follows:

> In a book containing 148 numbers (hymns, anthems, cantatas, oratorios) all of them in manuscript, written for the bass in the orchestra, yet containing the words of the compositions, I find not only standard works of the time but original compositions for chorus and orchestra. Among these are:
>
> Fair art thou Harmonie.
> Who hath unveiled the mysteries of Harmonie?
> Blest Be Ye Goodly.
> To whom now sounds the festal peal.
> O beauteous Harmonie.
> Gone is all my strength.
> Praise the Lord, Jerusalem.
> Harmonie Thou Fairest.
> So Children, What can further bind you?
> Hail, Hail, Hail to the lamb.
> Harmonie, listless as to place, change.

THE LABYRINTH

All Hail to thee, O Day. (This greeting was written for the Harmonie Fest of the year 1830.)
Arise Harmonie, be of good cheer. (1833)

It is proper to conclude the significant comments of Mr. Duss upon Harmonist music by quoting his final reference in that connection to the two greatest of all Harmonists—George and Frederick Rapp.

Reverting once more to the early days: George Rapp wrote many hymns. He was a poet in the manner born, so to speak; this, together with his inclination to mysticism, placed him in a field beyond the ken of ordinary mortals. But he did not essay to compose music. Frederick wrote both religious and secular poetry and music; what became of it nobody knows, except the one hymn, No. 134 in the Hymnal *Children in Friendship*. He collaborated with Geo. Rapp in writing the Society's favorite hymn No. 163 *Harmonie Thou Brother State*. It is a fine mixture of the mystic and the practical—the hand of each is readily discerned.

Through the genius and industry of Mr. Duss, an attractive music book of twenty-five pages is available, of which the title page is fully explanatory.

1824   THE HARMONIE   1924

COLLECTION OF COMPOSITIONS

By Various Heads of The Harmony Society

Frederick Rapp	Trustee	A. D.	1805-1834
George Rapp	Trustee	A. D.	1834-1847
Jacob Henrici	Trustee	A. D.	1847-1892
John S. Duss	Trustee	A. D.	1890-1903

"HARMONIE THOU FLOWER FAIR"
(Centennial Ode)

"CHILDREN OF FRIENDSHIP"

"THE LORD'S PRAYER"
German and English Text

"O COME ALL YE FAITHFUL"

"YE GENTLE HARMONITES"
German and English Text

"GLORIA FROM MASS IN HONOR OF ST. VERONICA"
Latin and English Text

ECONOMY CENTENNIAL_____SOUVENIR EDITION

Published by the Economy Centennial Association
June—1924

[84]

THE BUILDERS OF THE LABYRINTH

The great music hall of the Harmony Society as it still stands at Economy has already been described.

It is hoped that this somewhat casual summary will serve to indicate something of the meaning and importance of music in the Harmony Society. It was vital to their work and worship. Often the Harmony band led large processions of harvesters—both men and women—to the fields and regaled them with inspiring strains while they swung their sickles in rhythmic unison. They enjoyed it in field and workshop, in orchard and vineyard, and at the Labyrinth; as well as in home and church and public hall. How truly it integrated their fundamental conception of harmony! We may well believe that their "souls were filled with celestial harmony" while they found "solace and enjoyment in the melody of earth."

THE CEMETERY

THE old Rappite Cemetery, commonly known as the German Grave Yard, still maintained in the heart of New Harmony substantially as the Rappites left it, is a solemn material symbol of their faith and devotion. 230 members of the Harmony Society passed away during the ten years they were in Indiana, from 1814 to 1824. The death rate was very high during their early years here because of the prevalence of fever and ague along the Wabash in those pioneer days. However, they seem to have conquered these unhealthful conditions for during their last year there were only two deaths.

Each of the 230 who died was laid away at early twilight with simple ceremony by Father Rapp and a few of the elders of the community. No time was lost for funeral obsequies, and apparently there was no ostentatious mourning. As soon as the coffin was lowered, the leader (Father Rapp) repeated I Peter 1:24-25:

> For all flesh is as grass, and all the glory of man as the flower of grass. The grass withereth and the flower thereof falleth away. But the word of the Lord endureth forever.

Then he cast a handful of flowers upon the coffin and each one attending did the same. The coffin was a plain wooden box, unlined and unadorned.

It was not expected that this last resting place would be long occupied. They were left at rest under the flowers as symbols of their belief in an early resurrection. There were no external decorations for any of the graves or for the cemetery as a whole. They were grassed over, plain and level, all alike, equal in death as in life. No stones were placed; there were no mounds or markers, no relics or tokens of a tomb. This solemn resting place was preserved as sacred ground.

When the estate of Harmonie was transferred to Robert Owen, the cemetery passed with the rest of the property in the general deed. However, a separate bond was required of Robert Owen, executed April 25, 1825, in which he bound himself and "his heirs, executors, administrators, or assigns to protect or cause to be protected from all and every interference and annoyance in whatsoever shape or manner it may be, nor to disturb, nor suffer to be disturbed in no manner or wise, the graveyard" —*during the full term of twenty years from this date* and "to keep the post and rail fence as it now stands, in good repair during said term."

THE BUILDERS OF THE LABYRINTH

At the expiration of the twenty years, the millennium had not come, and something had to be done about the cemetery. Father Rapp was still living, 87 years of age. He brought about the purchase of the cemetery in 1845 so that it again came into possession of the Harmony Society all in one complete unit. It had been partly divided into burial lots. It then continued in the ownership of the Harmony Society all in one plot of ground as they had left it in 1825.

When the old brick church was being torn down in 1874, after serious damage from a storm, the Harmony Society sent two trustees back to New Harmony from Economy and on September 29, 1874, they entered into a new arrangement for the permanent preservation of the cemetery in its original form. Purchasing the ground upon which the old church stood they conveyed it to the town of New Harmony, or rather to Harmony Township, for the purpose of maintaining a public school building thereon. They also gave to the township $2,000.00 to be used in erecting the building, together with some of the brick, stone, and timber that was salvaged from the old building. However, they reserved enough bricks to erect the strong wall that now surrounds the cemetery.

This being done, they executed an indenture in the form of a conditional grant or conveyance of the church ground to Harmony Township for the purpose of maintaining a school building thereon with the condition that the said Harmony Township "will from time to time, and at all times hereinafter take good and proper care, and keep in proper condition the German Grave Yard aforesaid, and protect and guard the same from all trespasses and mutilation of the trees on the same." It provided further "that upon breach of these conditions, by neglect or failure in the performance of the duties herein required, this conveyance shall become null and void and of no effect. And it shall thereupon be right and lawful for the said first party, or their heirs or successors in said trust, or the heirs or successors of the survivors of them to re-enter upon and hold said premises [the church (now school) grounds] to them, their heirs or successors in said trust, or assigns, forever."

And so the old cemetery has stood legally from that day under the care of Harmony School Township, but with the title and full right of ownership remaining in the Harmony Society, and the church (now, school) ground remaining only in the conditional ownership of the township.

The Harmony Society was dissolved in 1906 and since then has had no corporate existence. By judgment of the Circuit Court of

Posey County, in May, 1941, the cemetery passed into complete ownership and control of the State of Indiana as a part of the New Harmony
Memorial. Needless to say, it will be maintained perpetually as the
old Rappite Cemetery—a distinct unit of historic New Harmony—
where 230 of the original founders of the community are sleeping
under the flowers, awaiting the coming of the millennium.

This historic old cemetery gains additional memorial significance
from the fact that it contains also a group of well defined Indian
mounds. Some of these mounds were excavated by scientists of the
Owen regime—the first archaeological researches of that kind made in
North America west of the Alleghanies. The Rappites respected this
ancient burial ground and were unwilling to disturb the last resting
place of prehistoric men. That is no doubt the reason why they placed
their own cemetery there in the very heart of their little town, making
it large enough to include these mounds and leave sufficient space for
their own interments near by. Thus a fine spiritual kinship is made
manifest—the Harmonist under the flowers, awaiting the millennium;
the Indian with his faithful dog and bow, ready for the Happy Hunting
Ground beyond the Milky Way. The Happy Hunting Ground was
just as real to the simple aborigine as the millennium was to the reverent
Harmonist.

ENTRANCE TO RAPPITE CEMETERY

𝔄𝔭𝔭𝔢𝔫𝔡𝔦𝔵

RESUME OF HARMONIST HISTORY

THE Harmony Society originated in the preaching of George Rapp at the little town of Iptingen in Wurttemberg, Germany. Beginning in 1787 in his 30th year, he preached a Separatist doctrine of socialized religion based upon the older Pietism. He organized a compact band of devoted followers and when they suffered persecution because of their firmly expressed religious convictions they followed him as a homogeneous group to America in 1803-4 to the number of about 600.

A colony, which they named Harmonie, was established in Butler County, Pennsylvania, about 25 miles northwest of Pittsburgh 12 miles from the Ohio River. There on February 15, 1805, they formed themselves into a communal organization, which they named the Harmony Society.

After ten years of prosperity in this home in the New World they sought a more favorable location, farther west on a navigable stream. Some 30,000 acres was purchased on the lower Wabash in what is now Posey County, Indiana, in 1814, and a new settlement was formed there which they also named Harmonie. There they prospered exceedingly for ten years and then sold the community in 1824— $150,000.00 for the land and $40,000.00 for some selected personal property—to Robert Owen who had attained wide fame as an industrial and social revolutionist in New Lanark, Scotland. He named the community New Harmony and began an experiment in educational socialization through a Community of Equality, which consisted of an entirely different and a very heterogeneous group.

The Rappites, as the members of the Harmony Society came to be known soon afterwards in history, all moved to a new settlement in 1824-25 in Beaver County, Pennsylvania, on the Ohio River—18 miles north of Pittsburgh. They numbered at that time about 900 members. 230 had died while they were in Harmonie on the Wabash but an accession of 130 new members had come to them from their old neighborhood in Wurttemberg and some had been taken in through probation.

This new colony was named Economy. They remained there until the final dissolution of the Harmony Society in 1906. It existed as an organization for just 101 years. A few of their old buildings still stand at the site of their first colony in Harmonie (now Harmony), Pennsylvania. A great many of them are preserved in their Harmonie on the Wabash (now New Harmony) and in Economy, Pennsylvania (now Ambridge).

It may be stated here as the official view of the New Harmony Memorial Movement that the name of the Harmonist settlement on the Wabash should always be spelled Harmonie and pronounced Harmonèè. That was the way the Harmonists themselves always spelled and pronounced it. Using it in that way distinguishes it fittingly in connection with its later characterization as the New Harmony of the Owenites. Nearly all early historical writers spelled it Harmonie, although it is found interchanged occasionally with Harmony, which was adopted by the U. S. Post Office Department.

The significance of the spelling and pronunciation of Harmonie is given emphasis by John S. Duss in a written statement, August 31, 1941:

> There is no question as to the use of HARMONIE whenever and wherever occasion arises. It is the name the Harmony Society gave to the first settlement in Butler County, Pa., and to the second settlement on the Wabash in Indiana.
>
> It is especially appropriate because the members of the Harmony Society in speaking of the Society invariably called it "Die Harmonie" (The Harmony)—in other words, this and that happened in HARMONIE or things were done thus and so in HARMONIE. The term was all-embracing, to wit: the people, their principles, mode of life, and their town and acres. A wonderful word indeed, and a continual reminder and talisman in regard to the daily life of the members. Furthermore the accent on the last syllable makes the word longer, of heavier import, and preferable from the standpoint of euphony or music.

INSTITUTIONAL MEMORIAL EXERCISES

In harmony with the spirit of this treatise, regular exercises are being instituted for the memorialization of the reverence and mysticism of the founders of Harmonie. A Posey County Ministerial Memorial Auxiliary has been formed as a voluntary association for this purpose. It conducts religious ceremonies regularly at stated intervals on Sunday afternoons throughout the tourist season on spots that are peculiarily suggestive of spiritual features of Harmonist life. The sites chosen for these services are the old Rappite Cemetery, the church ground before the millennial arch, and the foreground of the Labyrinth.

This Memorial Auxiliary consists of ministers of the Gospel of all religious denominations who live or preach in Posey County. It assumes responsibility for assigning one or more ministers to have charge of each of the ceremonies. During the season of 1941 services were held as follows—on August 10, Rev. L. N. Campbell, Pastor of the New Harmony Methodist Church, assisted by Dr. W. L. Jones, District Superintendent of the Evansville District, conducted the first service in the Rappite Cemetery; on September 14, Rev. Cecil Atkinson, Pastor of the First Presbyterian Church of Mt. Vernon, directed the service at the millennial arch; and on October 12, Rev. S. J. Skelton of the Methodist Church of New Harmony concluded the series for this season on the foreground of the Labyrinth under the big elm tree.

At each of these services, appropriate music was rendered by members of various church choirs and of the Grace Golden Music Guild of New Harmony. Everyone present felt the indefinable contagion of this unique assemblage of associations. By such direct contact with consecrated sites through the eyes and through the feet, the history and symbolism that inhere in them become expressive of spiritual values that never die. The songs that were sung and the words that were spoken breathed a genuine memorial spirit.

Some well known Rappite songs were rendered. With this modest beginning, the reproduction of the distinctive music of the Rappites is being made an important Memorial feature. Through choral groups, orchestras and bands, as well as by electrical transcription and movietone, the spirit of the devoted Harmonists may be made vocal again on the very places and in the very buildings where their voices and their hand-made musical instruments were often heard.

THE LABYRINTH

For the purpose of cultivating appreciation of the Harmonious-Spirit (Harmonische-Geist) of the founders of Harmonie, the observance of their annual Harvest Home Festival will be made an institutional Memorial feature. Plans are in progress in correlation with the Indiana Farm Bureau, as an auxiliary of the New Harmony Memorial Commission, to establish this institution in August 1942, by a day of feasting and music after the manner in which that festive occasion was regularly observed by the Harmonists. It will constitute a recognition of the reverent gratitude of those pious people to an all wise Providence for the rewards they enjoyed from the fruitfulness of the soil which they cultivated so well—a fitting celebration both of their work and their worship.

Nothing could be more significant in this connection than the restoration of the Rappite Kingdom of Flowers. A project was launched at the beginning of the Memorial Movement that looks toward the beautification of the entire town of New Harmony as a modern realm of flowers. It was made so in the very beginning of its existence as a town by the Rappite practice of cultivating fine flowers on every lot and garden, as well as within the houses and factories of the entire community, as explained in another part of this brochure.

In order to restore this fragrant custom, an Annual Flower Day has been instituted as a regular Memorial project and observed May 6, 1939, May 7, 1940, and May 14, 1941. By the expert sponsorship of the Horticultural Department of Purdue University, assisted by the Indiana Garden Club, the programs and exercises of this annual day are devoted to the encouragement and direction of floral culture in every home, as well as in the community at large. The Conservation Club of New Harmony is in direct charge of the project under the general auspices of the New Harmony Memorial Commission. The Commission furnishes seeds and young plants. A flower exchange and a flower show are special features.

Through the awakened interest of all the people of New Harmony, there will ultimately come the complete inauguration of a symbolical Kingdom of Flowers which will make of the entire community one great Memorial unit. Of course, this is correlated fittingly with the Golden Rain Tree Festival which is a Memorial observance of the Owenite regime. Trees of Golden Rain, first known as Gate Trees, were introduced here in the days of the *Community of Equality* by William Maclure and Thomas Say.

APPENDIX

PANEL INSCRIPTIONS

BASED upon the considerations involved in the facts and sentiments presented in this brochure, the restoration of the Labyrinth of the Harmony Society is offered to the world with all the significance that may be attached to it. Here the thoughful pilgrim may indulge his reflective fancy to his heart's content. For the sober minded, it may carry the most profound suggestions of the difficult and uncertain ways of life, and it may inspire the hope that notwithstanding the devious ways every pilgrim will have to tread, he may find the path to a happy ending.

In any event, it is certain that this Labyrinth embodies no token of the grave. It will not inspire fears of hideous monsters, jealous queens, or musty tombs of kings and crocodiles. Rather its pleasing aspects should bring edifying reflections, both of an earthly and heavenly nature in keeping with the idealistic purposes upon which the New Harmony Memorial is based and in harmony with the spiritual conceptions of the founders of Harmonie.

The inscriptions on the panels of the temple are typically Harmonian. They are taken mainly from the *Thoughts* of Father Rapp.

> George Rapp, Founder of the Harmony Society, born 1757, died 1847.
>
> Harmonie, Penna. Founded 1804. Harmonie, Ind. Founded 1814. Economy, Pa. Founded 1824.
>
> What a harmonious people! In safety thou reachest the lofty summit, where few can travel, and from which many fall, or become lost and bewildered in the labyrinth of the artificial philosophy of the world.
>
> And the multitude of them that believed were of one heart and one soul; neither said any of them that aught of the things which he possessed was his own; but they had all things common.—Acts IV:32.
>
> The true principles of religion and the prudent regulations of industry and economy, by their united influence, produce a *heaven upon earth—a true Harmony*.
>
> Let not the sun go down upon your wrath.
>
> Love to God above all and to thy neighbor as thyself.
>
> A harmonious and united society of men may be said to be a Kingdom of God.
>
> We endure and suffer, labor and toil, sow and reap, with and for each other.
>
> Under this serene sky and friendly clime, will the fruits of noble achievements and wholesome constitutions come to greater maturity.

THE LABYRINTH

God requires no more of any human being than one man of honour and reputation requires of another.

The Creator of the Universe has always in view the happiness of all the human race.

The golden treasure of this world, to those who know how to preserve it, is Friendship.

The day of the Lord is drawing near, and will dominate over all that is high, and humiliate all which is lofty.

Again a day is passed and a step made nearer the end.

Our time runs away and the joys of heaven are our reward.

MILLENNIAL ARCH (ROSE DOOR)